*For Dave & Gerry —
with lasting friendship*

Harold
June 1979

Grateful acknowledgement is made to the following publications in which most of the poems in this book originally appeared or were reprinted:

Aesop's Feast; The Agni Review; "Mrs. Marsden" © 1968 by The Antioch Review, Inc. First published by *The Antioch Review*, vol. 28, no. 3, fall 1968; *Approach;* "I Don't Remember", which appeared in Vol. IV, no. 2 of *Arts in Society* is being published with the permission of the editors; *Bachy; The Beloit Poetry Journal; The Carleton Miscellany; Caryatid;* "A Voice in the Rapids," "Rich Man, Poor Man", "They" and "Mrs. Northcross" reprinted, courtesy of the *Chicago Tribune; The Colorado Quarterly; Concerning Poetry;* "Brother" reprinted with the permission of the Macmillian Publishing Co., Inc. from *Beasts in Clothes* by Harold Witt, © Harold Witt, 1959, 1961. Originally appeared in *Contact; Counter/Measures; Crazy Horse; December; The Dragonfly; Dryad; Everyman; The Florida Review; The Greenfield Review; Gryphon; Happiness Holding Tank; Hearse;* and thanks to E. V. Griffith, *Hearse Press,* for the publication of *Winesburg by the Sea: A Preview,* 1970, in which various poems were reprinted; *Hiram Poetry Review; The Hudson Review; In a Nutshell; The Iowa Review; King James Review; The Massachusetts Review; Michigan Quarterly Review; The Midwest Quarterly; New Laurel Review; New Letters; The New Orleans Review; The New Republic; New Salt Creek Reader; The New York Times* for "Now in November" © 1965 by The New York Times Company. Reprinted by permission. Also reprinted in *Family Tree,* © 1967 by the World Publishing Company; *The New Yorker; Northeast; Northwest Review; Pebble;* And thanks to Greg Kuzma, *Best Cellar Press,* for publication of *Pop. by 1940: 40,000,* in which several of the poems were reprinted or first appeared; *The Periodical Lunch; Per/Se; Perspective; Poet Lore; Poetry* for "Photograph of Ghosts", reprinted in *Superman Unbound* by Harold Witt, *The New Orleans Poetry Journal,* 1956; *The Poetry Bag; Poetry Northwest; Poetry NOW; Poetry: People; Prairie Schooner; Quartet Magazine; The Reporter; Saturday Review* for "Ebersoles' Potato Chips" © 1969, Saturday Review, Inc., and "Leslie Aumaire" © 1966, Saturday Review, Inc., the latter reprinted in *People in Poetry* © The Macmillan Co., 1969, and *Microcosm: College and the World,* © 1972, Harcourt Brace Jovanovich Inc.; *Seizure Magazine, The Shore Review; The Smith; South; Southern Humanities Review; Southern Poetry Review; Southwest Review; The Sparrow Magazine; The Sunstone Review; Tennessee Poetry Journal; Three Rivers Poetry Journal; Twigs; Two Feet of Poetry; University of Tampa Poetry Review;* "The Bank of Italy," "This is KFI, Los Angeles" and "Homework" © 1976 by Olivant Press. Published in WEID *The Sensibility Revue,* vol. IX; *West Coast Poetry Review; Wind; The Windless Orchard; The Wormwood Review; Yankee; Zahir.* "Gettysburg" in *Family in the Forest* © 1956 by Harold Witt, The Porpoise Bookshop, Peregrine Press; "Aunts and Uncles 2 & 3" originally published by *The New Yorker* and "Hand on the Gun", originally published by *Poetry Northwest* reprinted in *A Western Sampler* © 1963 by The Talisman Press; "Veil of Perfume", originally published by *The Beloit Poetry Journal,* reprinted in *The Death of Venus* by Harold Witt, © 1958 The Golden Quill Press; "Stationery. Cards. Notions. Books.", originally published by *Poetry NOW,* reprinted in *The Pushcart Prize: Best of the Small Presses* © 1976 by The Pushcart Book Press.

Typography by *The Chowder Review.*

WINESBURG BY THE SEA

poems

Harold Witt

for my children

"Those who cannot remember the past
are condemned to repeat it."
--- George Santayana

"The past is not dead; it is not even past."

--- William Faulkner

Library of Congress Cataloging in Publication Data

Witt, Harold.
   Winesburg by the sea.

   I. Title.
PS3545.19257W5   811'.5'4   78-2924
ISBN 0-914476-70-X
ISBN 0-914476-71-8 pbk.

Copyright © 1979 by Harold Witt

Photo by Eric Witt

THORP SPRINGS PRESS
3414 Robinson Avenue
Austin, Texas 78722

NOW IN NOVEMBER

Now in November, ten years after then,
fragility grown to bigness, Emily runs
homeward from fractions with her violin,
her hair as brilliant as the turning oaks,
followed by Eric vivid in his shirt.

Flitting behind them, sparrows tip with sun
and peck the pyracanthas' berried arcs.
I didn't guess this autumn lesson when
I heard them, dimly, cry in early darks ---
meanings of time we learn only from children,

how they come in from the arrowy sun,
leaves falling behind them, as I ran once,
and the glad dog does a delicate dance,
their "Oh OK," when asked how school was,
then off to try their balance on a fence.

I hear, as evening deepens, acorns thud
from the darkening tree they're climbing in
against a glow that slowly streaks with blood,
and on that golden bough I am the one
who hears my vanished father call me home.

TABLE OF CONTENTS

Now in November	5
I: ELEMENTARY EDUCATION	
Winesburg by the Sea	11
Cock-a-Doodle-Doo	12
Martin's Texas Tamales	13
Photograph of Ghosts	13
Catalina	14
The Cruel Sea	15
Again, Again	15
Fessendens'	16
Confetti	17
A Voice in the Rapids	17
Bed Harding's Flying Machine	18
The Depression	19
Ear	19
Marjorie	20
Alice White	20
Hired Girls	21
I Don't Remember	21
Saturday Nights and Sunday Mornings	22
Miss Herring	23
Jealousy	23
Brother	24
Hand on the Gun	24
Orange	25
Veil of Perfume	25
Aunt Nettie	26
Uncles in the Orchard	27
Aunts and Uncles	27
Sundays at Uncle Earl's	28
Rich Man, Poor Man	29
The Science They Breathed	30
Gettysburg	30
I Touched the Hand That Shook the Hand of Lincoln	31
Under the Roses	32
Veterans	32
Everett	33
What She Said	34
The Johnson Smith & Company	34
Miss Hale's	35
Like Any Boy	36
Rumble Seat	36
Jump Rope	37
Tearful Occasions:	
Peroxide	38
Perspective	38
Desperate Desmond	39
Marilyn's Father	39
Joseph Horwitz	40
Elementary Education	40
Larry Worth	41
Heck Quinn	42
Bones	43
Life in the Tomb	43
O Pioneers!	44
Two Grandmothers:	
Hannah	44
Sarah	45

Topless	46
Miss Platt	47
Birch Street	48
The Bank of Italy	49
Green Orchard	50

II: WEST EIGHTEENTH

West Eighteenth	51
Black Anecdote	52
The Vegetable Man	53
Neighbors	53
Mrs. Marsden	54
They	54
Mrs. Small	55
Mr. Small	55
S.(our) M.(ilk) Lovett	56
Ebersoles' Potato Chips	56
Elaine Farquhar	57
Warm Days	58
The Day the Governor Played Ball	58
Under the Eucalyptus	59
Hiroshima	60
Dr. Earl Blood, The Painless Dentist	60
Felicia Best	61
Dr. Farsdale	61
Harry Chin, Chinese Herbalist	62
The Seth Thomas	63
German,	63
Zelda Keith	64
This Is K.F.I., Los Angeles	65
Junior	66
Time in the Evening	67
Nervous Breakdown	68
Little Bobby	68
Maud Winters' Swedish Massage Salon	69
Mr. Mueller	70
Eddie Weismann	70
Mr. Virgo	71
Those Veaches	72
Screaming on Seventeenth	72
Next Door	73
The Symbol	74
The Times	75
Aunt Lucy	76
Past Ten O'Clock	77

III: COMING HOME FROM THE MOVIES

Rewrite	78
The Jazz Singer	79
Tom Mix	80
Those Times When Richard Barthelmess Went Up	80
Our Gang	81
Those Busby Berkeley Musicals	82
Mae West	82
Tarzan	83
Godiva Ridden	83
And Greened My Twelfth, Most Verdant Summer	84
The Annunciation	84
The First Time	84
At the Broadway	85

High Places:	
Lost Horizon	86
Mutiny on the Bounty	86
Wuthering Heights	86
Homework	87
The Clever Studio	88
Sugar and Spice	88
Complaint	89
Lady Chatterley's Lover	90
Robert Taylor	90
The Marx Brothers	91
Beyond the Rainbow	91
Love Affair	92
The Hurricane	92
Dark Victory	93
Coming Home from the Movies	94
Solo	94
Starting at Thirteen	95
Past Bean Fields	96
In Those Days	96
Ars Gratia Artis	97
It Took a Long Time	98
Gone with the Wind	99
When I Finally Went to MGM	100
IV: HOLD IT	
Pop. by 1970: 40,000	101
Passing Through	102
Vivian	103
Belle Small	104
Doc Clark	105
Oswald Shrader	106
Mrs. Nice at the Talkies	107
Grandma Folkston	107
Etta Johnson	108
Elmer Slater	109
Marianne Cox	110
Deacon Ennart	110
Mary Meechum	111
Widow Willis, the Cat Lady	112
Bubbles	112
Johnny Walsh, Checkered Cab Co.	113
A Man from the Freight	114
Slim the Janitor	114
The Santa Ana Wind	115
Mr. Foote, Postman	116
Joseph and Mary Pilford	117
Robert Furness, Doctor of Divinity	118
Edith Furness, Minister's Wife	119
Touchdown Brown, Dept. of Sanitation	119
Ramona Lopez	120
Clarence Holmes, Attorney at Law	121
Carlotta Seyrig, Palm Readings	122
A Faithful Husband	122
Abby Arthenot, Waitress	123
The Golfer	124
Daisy Hemingway, Dressmaking & Alterations	125
Angel Rodriguez	125
Mile High Miles	126
K-O-R-E, The Voice of the Citrus Empire	127

Golden Gloves	127
Ernest J. Licht, Physician & Surgeon	128
Tobacco. Candy. Magazines	128
Arthur Couchay's Ladies' Apparel	129
Bessie's Beautie Shoppe	130
Millie's Millinery	130
Zeta Goff, Chiropodist	131
The Arkansas Travelers	132
Mike Allman	133
Bert Perkings, Station Master	133
Number Please	134
Karl Bower, Nurseryman	134
Mrs. Wright	134
Stationery. Cards. Notions. Books.	135
Helen Payne, Spotter	136
Fay Purvis	136
I.I. Augen, Optometrist	137
The Projectionist	138
Otto Uhr, Watch Repair	138
"Dummy" Randall	139
Margo Martine, Studio of the Dance	140
Georgina Gorman, R.N.	140
Chest 46", Waist 32", Biceps 18½"	141
Lura O'Leary	142
Ian di Lanzo	142
Nancy Van Deusen	143
Henna Vinal, Birdwatcher	144
Adam Crabtree, Beekeeper	145
"Rubens" Jones	146
Al Booster, Chamber of Commerce	146
Mad Mady	147
Rev. X. Burns McDermott	147
Hattie King	148
Flower World, L.P. Bloom, Prop.	149
Percy Tilg, Mortician	149
V: CLASS PICTURES	
Asked Back	151
Miss Dancey	152
Leslie Aumaire	152
Jesus Lopez	153
Ben-Hur	154
Mrs. Grook	154
Norma	155
Miss Dark	155
Dolores Knight	156
World History	157
Mr. Byron Jarvis	158
Über Alles	158
Rex Wishnevski	159
Physics	160
Mr. Music	160
Rita Rubio	161
Jack Henry	162
José Ramirez	162
Tom White	163
That Kid	163
Leon Hendrixon	164
Dan Anderson	165
Lee Zorn	165
C.B. "Mathew" Brady	166

Janet and Howard Darling	167
All Star	168

VI: GAP

My Brother Made Model Airplanes	169
Oasis	170
Gap	170
Citrus Heights	171
Edward Morgan Barry	172
Our Town	172
Double Date	173
In the Basement of the Carnegie Library	174
Mrs. Northcross	174
Mlle. Smith	175
Miss Bagley	176
Judith Lovelace, M.A.	176
Dr. Tyger	177
Field Trips: Geology 1 & 2	178
Mrs. Oates	178
Social Conscience	179
Rosemary or Jasmine	179
Richard McGregor	180
Maryjo Malone	181
The Famous Poet	181
Chalice	182
The Stream	183
When No One Else Had Ever Been Eighteen	183
Feeling Surreal	184
From Aardvark to Zymurgy	184
Heigho Silver	185

VII: REMEMBER PEARL HARBOR

Places, Everyone	187
The Only Trouble	188
Communion	189
Our World	189
Norwalk	190
Remember Pearl Harbor	190
Steve Yamamoto	191
Edgar Nielson	192
My Sudden Cousin, My Sanguine Minister, and The Cruelty of Conviction	193
Conscientious Objector	194
Fires	194
Dressed for an Occasion	195
Eyes	196
Brothers	196
Now They Work In Banks	197
Oohing the Umlaut	198
1938----	198
I Find Time	200
Aunt Anna Marie Hayes	201
Golden Wedding	202
Later	203
Home Movies at Newport	204

Section One: ELEMENTARY EDUCATION

WINESBURG BY THE SEA

I thought Winesburg somewhere else but I lived in it,
my own Spoon River on the California coast,
no Virgil to show me around and to point out
in that bright darkness, the lesson of the lost.

I read of Main Street as a midwest place ---
An American Tragedy happened far to the east,
figures of old art on Keats's vase
no less remote than those tales or more antique.

Didn't I walk under palms in an air that blossomed
huge pink hibiscuses and poppies for the bees,
how could minds be anything but open
so close to sunset and the rich realm of the seas?

I had to go away and to look back like Orpheus
or Lot's wife turned to salt before I could see
how it really was, from one point of view glorious,
from another, hell itself, and damned past pity.

COCK-A-DOODLE-DOO

The rooster in this suburb crows me back
--- no blue was ever cobalt as those skies,
cannas couldn't have burst as bright as those ---
to waking in a boy's world of surmise,
a block of lawns, trees, cats, dogs, bungalows ---

even the word's gone now for wooden homes
with porchswing afternoons of lemonade;
we hadn't heard of suburbs, lived near town
where gingham witches clucked, whose gnarled hands sprayed
grain to the cock and hens, and the iceman came,

liquid diamonds leaking from his truck,
and tonged a cube of winter on his back.
Someone might have moved from a Main Street mansion ---
come on, Jim, Bill, Arthur, come on, Dick,
let's see if a skeleton key'll fit the lock ---

it does, and sneakered boys intrude
on parquet floors, a stairway curving up
to bedrooms, and real tile around the tubs,
a shower --- hey, someone left some soap ---
then know, by veils of blue cigarry smoke

hanging in the hall we aren't alone;
with hearts in bellies, stirred-by-terror hair
we're down the dusty bannister and gone ...
to dig a clubhouse in the vacant lot
or build a tent for secrets on the lawn:

Touch a toad, you'll break out into warts
In Africa they don't wear any clothes
I've seen your sister and she's getting tits
If you do catch warts you can cure them with potatoes
Why don't we try to swipe some cigarettes?

We're up in prickly cedars looking down,
skating the edge of everything there is
until our handlebars have learned the town,
until there's nothing left of innocence
but lower marks of height we've soon outgrown.

And brightness fades like smoke words from the air
with the Green Hornet and Tom Sawyer's fence,
multiplicities of what was rare
obscure us from our early vividness ---
unless some bird of dawning crows it clear.

MARTIN'S TEXAS TAMALES

My mother drives us as I lean from mohair
in the square Buick to the other side of town ---
we turn a corner at a grocery store,
I look the fanpalmed street both up and down
though I have been here many times before.

I've passed this gingerbread, these stormwarped porches,
the paintpeeled, useless shutters hung askew,
the little dogs exploding on the lawns
into big barks as we go driving through
poor people's twilight where there are no dawns ---

it's always six o'clock and time for supper,
with broken trikes and wagons left along
the root cracked sidewalk; there is a small
sign on a palmtree before the house we stop at,
a onetime mansion, yellow as Chagall.

The handlettered sign spells MARTIN'S TEXAS TAMALES ---
my welldressed mother goes up to the bulging door
and a dark lady in a night black shawl
flashes whitetoothed smiles I can see from the car,
takes the pan she's handed and after a while

brings it back, makes change, and that is all ---
except the still there smell through yesterday's paper
of warm tamales near me on the seat ---
life, that mysterious Mexican memory shaper
has wrapped in husks some mix that's cornmeal sweet.

PHOTOGRAPH OF GHOSTS

Smiling with high coiffures and enormous
silken hats, my several aunts
and mother posed, graceful as sylphs
for this seabeach photograph

on fleshcolored sand whose bits of sticks and tar
are long since tideward drawn, and by the waves
engulfed, quite gone, like their long skirts
that flourish no more under the different sun.

Cruel photograph, to have caught them
exuberant and young, the one's hand at that
clear cameo, and the starched lacy stuff
at this one's throat, for an instant only.

Among them, resurrected, the dead sister shares
their two-dimensional moment, ephemerid
frailer than they who circle
but a little longer the bright helium sphere.

CATALINA

The island came close again,
somehow floated in
and lost the blur of distance
as if such mists could thin ---
its hills showed chapparal,
its harbor with a pier
had masted ships and bathers
in quaint suits splashing near.

Ladies in hats, with parasols
strolled boardwalk Avalon
accompanied by sailors
and dandy Sunday men ---
my mother and my father
rocked in a picnic boat;
I heard their drifting laughter,
I saw the starring light ---

while I walked the far mainland
too hazed for them to see,
my watch ticking tomorrow,
they lived bright yesterday ---
some dream lens over the water
had zoomed them out of time ---
Sunday on La Grande Jatte
focused beyond an eye ---

they so young, on honeymoon
and I older than they
trying to call them home
to my side of the sea ---
Mom, don't you remember,
and Dad --- I'm getting grey ---
as they spooned on Catalina
blue decades away.

THE CRUEL SEA

She sat me by the waves
and said now you stay there ---
and one broke over my head,
tugging me into the glare ---

I gasped and coughed out salt,
my sandpail swirled away
and I felt or thought I felt
sea things munch at my legs.

I had been left to die,
a lunch for the sharks and snails,
lipped by the cruel sea
of love's betrayal.

She ran to lift me out
laughing (who wanted a daughter)
I wanted to get you over
fear of the water.

And for years I dreamed I was dragged
into that ocean,
struggling to shore from the mouths
of her cold emotion.

AGAIN, AGAIN

Again, again I swim
in images of foam
down to the seadrowned town,
under the rim of brine.

I walk the sandribbed times
of saltscent, pelican
(his slack beak skims sardines)
the sea is green as limes.

I hold my breath between
the fishers on the pier
and find my father there,
a pole curved from his hand.

He smiles, he's winding in
a hooked lip dripping gems,
o-eyes, black, immense ---
the rest of it is fin.

It struggles among buckets,
it tugs at my childish eye
until I don't quite cry.
My father, blood on his knuckles,

slaps it into a creel.
The glittering agates rise,
sinker, hook and line
fly whizzing from the wheel.

I run the other way,
I never hear since then
Christ, fisher of men
except the cruel bait

arcs from my father's hand,
the fooled tail flaps
in a metaphor that gasps
in air where I first drowned.

FESSENDENS'

Once I went in, the eyeglassed geezer
smiled and winked and said, "Well what'll it be?
Soda pop or ice cream out of the freezer ---
or tell you what --- we're getting in next week
an Aunt Jemima doll, wound with a key.

She opens up her mouth and sings 'Susannah'
and does a dance and only costs a dime."
The old store smelled like overripe banana,
and spotting the counter on which Fessenden leaned
was fish blood being drunk by a big green fly.

"Oh please," I said, "will you save a doll for me?"
"Sure will. Now what do you want today?"
And I chose ropes of licorice, five for a penny,
and skipped out happy into the glare from the sea.
I asked him every time if he'd got that Mammy

and every time he said "What do you mean?"
and denied, with a face as sour as a pickle,
he'd ever mentioned a doll that sang a tune ---
and even when he gave me a cherry Popsicle
it dripped in the different sun
like blood from a wound.

CONFETTI

She said "There's Someone up in the sky
who's going to punish you for what you've done"
which was: stealing a box of confetti
from an open garage, abetted by Donald McMillan.
We'd tossed it up in the air and it fluttered along
the walks, the afternoon lawns, like snow on the bushes.
"You know your taking it was very wrong
and you're going to have to tell Mrs. Smith you took it."
We did. Mrs. Smith eight feet high
glowering out of her door, in glittering glasses,
said, however --- "Oh, that's all right
except you'd better clean up after your messes."
But though we quickly swept away our sin
it took years to stop expecting God to swoop down.

A VOICE IN THE RAPIDS

Tragedy wasn't Hamlet or Medea ---
of whom it would be a while before I heard ---
but my Aunt Clara, away in a horseless carriage
with her young husband --- just wed in the Methodist Church.

The way my mother told it, I could see them ---
she in a hat tied down with a blowing veil,
and he in a cap, bug goggles --- both of them laughing,
the road in those days hardly more than a trail.

They stopped at sunset somewhere up in the mountains ---
the odor of pine, and jays that probably squawked,
the green and white river swirling, gushing with fountains ---
bees must have buzzed in buttercups where they walked.

"And while Aunt Clara was cooking their wedding supper
over a fire her groom had happily made,
he decided to go for a little swim in the river,
stripped to his drawers --- into the cold cascade.

She heard him yell "Help! Help!" and heard him screaming ---
though thought it was only one of the jokes he played ---
but when he didn't come back she went down to the river,
stood on the bank and called, then crazily prayed.

Later they found his body, facedown and bloated ---
it took Aunt Clara five years to get over the shock ---
a tragedy --- " my mother said, and in that word
a voice in the rapids cries back from pitiless rock.

BEN HARDING'S FLYING MACHINE

As the thing with crisscrossed wires between its wings
went up like a halfbaked bird and then crashed down,
the men yelled "Get a horse" and the ladies tittered
but Ben Harding got out and bowed in his goggles and cap
and clasped his hands above his head in a sign of winning
and wasn't embittered.

Greeted with jokes on the street,
he went right on thinking and tinkered around
and once, on a porchswing, my mother (with eyes averted)
told (and she might have if his nails hadn't oozed grease)
that he'd asked her to marry him, and blurted
when she laughed no, "All right, you'll see, you'll see!"

Ben went home whistling and patiently twisted his wrenches
until even the stupidest cows had to agree
as a sound like a giant lawnmower ratcheted over
and their milk curdled, and dogs, terrified, peed,
that someone besides birds could fly and angels hover
and shine in the sky and suddenly pick up speed.

And Ben became famous and rich and was good to his mother,
giving her houses and servants and cars and gown after gown
from Paris (and never married) my mother said (with a sigh)
almost as if she wished instead of doubting she'd believed
he'd get off the ground, and high above town,
like Zeus with Leda, her sons had been conceived.

THE DEPRESSION

My father sometimes said we were going to the poor house
and nothing got my mother madder than that ---
I saw us leaving, with a few rags in the Buick ---
would they let me take along my cat?
My mother, furious, splotches on her neck,
shouted "Just because I bought a new spring hat!"

"Money don't grow on trees" was his next comment
and I saw orange trees, green with dollar bills,
neat and round in long rows at the ranch ---
then in my mother's voice the tone that chills
"Miser! Tightwad! Skinflint!"
and from her pretty face, a knifing glance.

He must have got rich quick. Morning glowed better.
We didn't pack up and move to the County Farm.
She kept the hat, and that night above the platter
of juicy beef generous Dad was carving
he said, as if nothing had been the matter,
"Eat every scrap.
Someplace kids are starving."

EAR

> "Lowell inherited wit and a love of poetry
> from his mother." —*The World Book*

"Whether we look or whether we listen,
We hear life murmur, or see it glisten" ---
my mother used to quote
on a what-is-so rare day
not much different
from this one.

She with her henna hair
and grey bearded James Russell Lowell
are both long gone and few remember
such old anthropomorphic poems ---
"Then Heaven tries the earth if it be in tune
And over it softly her warm ear lays."

Still though when this blue warmth happens
I once more am that small boy
running out from where my mother's finger
hisses testing the iron,
and looking up to where I'm sure there'll be
a giant ear descending from the sky.

MARJORIE

I was going to marry my cousin Marjorie ---
as pretty as any star in the rotogravure,
and I thought she loved me, the way she gave me candy
and those times she cuddled and kissed me I was sure ---

but she had a tall thin man she called a beau
who sometimes towsled my hair or playfully poked me.
"Clifford, you be nice," she smiled as she said
whenever he got too rough and might have provoked me.

Then one day my mother said, "Marjorie's eloped"
and I asked her what that meant and she only sighed
"Ran away and got married --- to Clifford, you know ---"
Then I knew she'd never be my bride

even if I should hurry up and grow,
but she was so beautiful, I could have cried.

ALICE WHITE

Blondly radiant, lighting the grey walk,
perfect as her name, came Alice White.
She stopped to skip the squares of hopscotch chalk
while I, my tongue too tied in knots to speak,
watched until she dazzled out of sight,
her pink bows bobbing as she danced along.
And I began to wobble, warm and weak,
as I sighed home, not knowing what was wrong.
Bigger kids in knickers might have whizzed
and squealed their wheels so she would have to stare,
or shaken up a Nehi till it fizzed
and popped the top to show what they could dare ---
but how could any little shrimp of five
let a goddess know he was alive.

HIRED GIRLS

Louella's hair, so black I had to pull it,
sitting on her tasselled flapper's lap ---
Naomi's sky blue eyes I liked to wink at,
Viola's legs that made a silken zip
crossing and uncrossing as we sat
at Grandpa's when I wasn't half a man ---

hired girls, who cleaned and did the dishes
but in the evenings joined the family group ---
a beautiful succession of pert swishes,
soft hair and eyes and lips, and beaded loop ---
the early stirrers of my manly wishes ---
how nice they smelled, and swelled like ripened fruit.

Sister big and virtuous as nuns,
they'd lift me up and say that I was cute ---
Naomi holding me, her honeybunch ---
she ran off later with some gangling lout ---
but I liked blonde Viola just as much
whose teeth winked brighter, in a redder mouth.

Blasé roué, by then an old Don Juan ---
no sooner had Viola left for good
than I went into sleek Ramona's room,
who let me play at typing on her bed,
and leaned beside me with such wild perfume
I felt a blood she never knew I had.

I DON'T REMEMBER

I don't remember why --- or what we did there ---
it may be my mother needed to get away ---
at the Barbara Worth Hotel in Santa Barbara
beside the mission sea for a weekend stay.

There might have been palmtrees, sunsets on the waves,
purple lantana hillsides, long colonnades ---
all I recall is the dark panelled lobby,
and a fluttering headline in a chill that still pervades.

Cold looks of crisis, silences of hurt,
some turmoil underneath that hardly rippled the nice ---
there might have been these, I feel as I think back
to a bed with a sheet turned down as neat as ice,

but the rest of that winter weekend when I was five
at the Barbara Worth with its darkness and lighted name
is a why and what of ones who no longer can drive
in the old car home to warmth from a lonely time.

SATURDAY NIGHTS AND SUNDAY MORNINGS

Saturday nights, dressed in our innocence,
my mother curled, my father's Homburg neat,
my brother and I both slicked with Vaseline
to keep our hair as polished as our feet,
we parked downtown, got out and shopped around
as regular as rituals repeat.

Salvation ladies shook their tambourines
and men in buttons tromboned for our sins ---
the windows showed us toys and dummy scenes ---
skirts that were up to knees or down to shins,
radios and all the latest things
for Easters, Christmases and Halloweens.

We never bought much, met at nine o'clock
in Uncle Peter's shoe store, Fourth and Main ---
my father smoked his White Owl at the back
and let me have the rich band for a ring ---
and after anecdotes among the smoke
we went on home the same way we had come.

That was our life.
I added up and learned to read between.
Then Sunday's funnies and the dressed up ride
to Sunday School to hear about a man
they said was crowned with thorns and crucified.
Once every week we nailed him up again.

MISS HERRING

Remembering Miss Herring, redhead who taught me to read,
her faintly freckled arm flashing like ivory,
eyes flashing; holding up card after card,
oh she was slender, beautiful and lively ---
peppery tempered, sending to the principal
bad boys who whispered, giddy girls with gum;
learning personified, intelligence invincible ---
old to me then, I see her now as young.
Mistress of alphabets, flashing DOG and CAT,
tall twenty-five, sylph in filmy green,
she flashes cards of knowledge back and back
and I can read her spelled out suffering ---
love's rage fading in a slow small town,
hating every child not her own.

JEALOUSY

The way I pictured jealousy was this:
an old vignette my mother often told ---
she and Aunt Lillie, the young and older sister,
strolling one Sunday
in some Dakota field

with Uncle Peter, a handsome bridegroom then,
when a monstrous bull loomed toward them hooving and
                                          snorting ---
careless of cowpies,
Uncle Peter escorting

both to the safety of an empty wagon
and helped my mother up and then his bride,
a flurry of flounces and her wide sash dragging ---
which may have been the worst mistake
of his life ---

in that mad second giving a hand to my mother
before he'd saved his palpitating wife ---
she never forgot, or forgave one or the other,
and always felt that horn
twist in her side ---

ghostly as the one that tore my brother
and gored and gored him since the age of five
when I was born, he imagined his darling mother
forsaking him
to bring me home alive.

BROTHER

Tandemed by him down Memory Lane, the gun
slung across his broad back, his blond
head bobbing, his hard calves pumping us beyond
the city limits to the country sun,
I was his brother, bothersome and young,
behind him on the bike's rack, holding on,
hearing the fence posts whiz and asking all
eager tediums a small brother can.
From manzanita in the river bed,
feathers white edged, eyed like frightened jewels,
topknots quavering, quail flew
and some dropped back into the bushes, dead ---
brother, hero, blond god, why do I see
murdered birds still bleeding in your eyes?

HAND ON THE GUN

Hand on the gun the day the cat died ---
my father's manly one,
veined and sinewed, touched the trigger,
eternity between

then and the first shot, the first sick kitten
blasted beyond.
Truth in the orchard, death by the mustard
yellow with bees and sun,

virile the jaw at every cocking;
straight from the eye that sighted
bullets tore five furs of pathos ---
life could never be righted.

Meowing at last, the pink-tongued mother
whose comfort I had known
twitched to a stillness tears and shaking
wouldn't wake her from.

"The cats were sick. We couldn't keep them,"
he said. "It had to be done,"
and I fell down forever, cold in that clover,
but took his assassin's hand.

ORANGE

A symmetry of segment takes me back ---
the seeded juicy acid smell of fruit
when the rind's knifed off, a thicker outer fact
revealing all the softness of the truth---
Dad's there in the orchard, and the skin
spins an organge ribbon from his blade ---
how lucky can you get to be the son
of someone hard as he and so arrayed
his capable copper buttons catch the sun
raying through the blossoms and the leaves ---
he stands in shade where water ditches run
blue as his smiling eyes, with glints of doves,
above the thirsting roots that spread beneath,
and hands the globe of sweetness down to me.

VEIL OF PERFUME

His black dog asleep by the emery wheel,
my ninety-year-old grandfather sits
sectioning an orange, juice trickling
into his stubborn goatee as he eats,

saying "*Schmeckt's gut,*" his straw-hatted
sons at lunch (like a Brueghel) before
the broad red door slid back that reveals
chicken feed spilled on a dirt floor.

Out of the barn's blue depths a Leghorn
crosses the dazzling gravel, idiotically,
red comb wobbling, pecking at rocks;
the sons doze under the umbrella tree.

My grandfather gets off the old Buick's fender;
the dog shakes himself licking my grandfather's
affectionately freckled hand. They go to look ---
walking the elliptic ditches of the orchard ---

at God's work, specking the leaves here with aphids,
stripping this branch bare, and there
hanging a whole tree with a veil of perfume
and bees and oranges, in the certain air.

AUNT NETTIE

A heart of gold was what I heard
about Aunt Nettie, big-boned, loud,
who pranced down ranch steps toward the car,
gossiping of sex and God.

Eyeglassed, in her apron, howled
that she'd been --- Halleluja! --- saved
(again) down at the river bed
where saints and sinners rolled and raved,

or inquired if we knew who
was doing what with who these days.
"Ain't we got fun?" --- she slapped a thigh ---
the sun through palmleaves flashed like blades,

the chickens pumped like golden hearts
on naked feet across the yard,
the windmill wheeled, the windcock turned,
new yolks bubbled in her barn.

She'd hand us tracts with Bible quotes
and redness warning to REPENT,
or tell us it was avocados
as healthful manna God had meant.

I thought she must have known His number
and between times of listening in
on neighbor ranches, through the static
chatted afternoons with Him,

she was so certain how we slipped,
and had His recipe for good ---
He must have told her who deserved
the bright sword of her righteous mood.

She cooked kind stews to serve the sick,
she could forgive, if He required,
but looking back I have to think
hearts of gold are sometimes hard.

UNCLES IN THE ORCHARD

You wouldn't have known they were the same men in the
                                          orchard ---
farting clowns under a tent of trees,
wearing Lee overalls that xed their backs ---
using censored words and taking pees,
they were like polite Huck Finns released
into a pristine auntless wilderness,

proud to be masculine beneath the leaves,
who had to hide it in a living room,
and sat so sanctimonious and meek
in pious pews hearing of sinners' doom ---
cracking jokes as they cracked walnut shells
and popped into shaven mouths the tender meats.

No, Uncle Joe, you weren't meant to be tamed
and led home by a lady, on a leash;
I saw you at your best, not very tall
but capable of anger as a beast ---
you must have seemed, before life made you small,
David with his sling, in dreams at least.

AUNTS AND UNCLES

1.
Where is Aunt Alice, Paderewski's pupil,
who smelled of mint, who winked across the keys
rings of seedpearl, turquoise, rings of opal,
whose smiles were music to my childish eyes,
who loosed, through the stuffiness were I was young,
sirens in Debussy's tonal seas,
who bent to better me with Bach among
surroundings inharmonious otherwise?
Deaf in a narrow parlor under grass,
silence at her marrow, beetles for a brain,
dead Aunt Alice lies pianoless,
safe from Mozart's joy or Chopin's pain,
and yet her smiles reverberate again,
her flesh-warm rings flash in my listening.

2.
Summer and winter my Aunt Lillie sat
chilled in her sunroom reading books of love,
her flesh bright clothed, her bones too deep for heat,
her odd, small body too entranced to move.
Vicarious heroine dancing tall and tense
through ballrooms of intrigue, the nymph of many beds,
she fled across romantic continents
while Uncle Peter multiplied like seeds
her planted cash, the money money breeds;
and she was richer than some princesses
but begged from fiction all her warmer needs
for real desire, for daring instances ---
lips at her icy ear, and hands to speed
her heart, not paper, while it still could beat.

3.
Now I am uncle, like homunculi
puny nephews, dwarfish nieces sport
comic around me, now instead of me
a later generation just as short
notes my mustachioed eccentricity
as once I stared at Uncle Peter's wart,
as, from the vantage of a lower eye,
normal faces frequently distort.
I view them not as children but as some
funny show of quick and charming freaks,
knowing my own enlargement looks to them
one of those natural, disturbing quirks
--- humorous animal or man from space ---
and neither dreams the other in his place.

SUNDAYS AT UNCLE EARL'S

Sundays at Uncle Earl's ---
who lived on a date-palmed road ---
Aunt Laura mixing the batter
in their little brown house in the grove ---

Gwendolyn --- a beauty ---
Jim --- who drew cartoons ---
and their dog, Woo, a wagging friend
old sun red afternoons ---

above the sofa, an Indian
on a horse at "The End of the Trail",
glinting even redder
as the light continued to fail.

All of us laughed in the kitchen
while the ticking waffles grew,
and that was the sweetest butter
and syrup we ever knew.

We talked --- Gwendolyn kissed me ---
Aunt Laura smiled and smiled
and Uncle Earl joked on and on
and Jim sat there and drew.

The stars came up to the windows ---
gems on velvet black ---
and we had to go home from the tasseled lamps ---
that long and dark way back.

RICH MAN, POOR MAN

Rich man, poor man, beggar man, thief ---
twiddling aunts went down our coats
counting out what we would be ---

Doctor, lawyer, merchant, chief ---
what little tickled men we were
perching on their silken knees

and in a perfumed cloud allowed
to dream of possibilities ---
weren't we pampered then and proud?

And some became what sweet aunts told
and some died early in a war
before our doting aunts were old

and some got rich and some stayed poor
while plump aunts shrank and shook and bent,
and some, who'd seemed so bright and sure

to go as far as buttons said
when bouncing aunts had counted there,
went mad, or broke, or drank instead.

THE SCIENCE THEY BREATHED

Sealed in that sweetness, nothing could touch them ---
nodding yes yes it's so true, so true
in the Health of the heat in the room like a tomb
and the Science they breathed saved them from seeing
pictures of danger where rugpatterns seethed ---
the mad eyed magician, the witch, and the tiger's
teethbaring smile not far beneath.

But Grandpa awoke and cried "Where's your head?"
on a battlefield screaming with cannons, he said,
the soldier beside him blown past believing
no one had died.

Then Aunt Alice spoke to him awfully softly
while Will's gold edged teeth completely agreed,
"You imagined it, Papa, death's not harmonious,
it's clearly erroneous,
and only exists as an unChristian creed."

GETTYSBURG

Smiling whitehaired, "My boy," he slapped a knee,
pulled out a worn thin watch and looked at me
while I got up from roses in the rug
and sat like expectation on his leg.
"Grandpa, tell me a story." "Well, my boy,
which would you like, the Civil War or Troy?"
"The Civil War," I said, " --- about the day
you died." "Not quite died but there I lay,
one lung shot out, voices overhead ---
'Leave him, he's dead,' 'Take him,' the other said ---
debating against a distant fusillade.
I saw their two blue figures blurred through blood,
oh my Lord, and couldn't wheeze a word.
Next I heard a wheel of water whirl,
soldiers cursing cards and I was on
a riverboat, maggots in my wound.
A man held up a cup I couldn't drink.
Where would you be, Harold, do you think,
if they had left me in that bloody mud?"
"Where would I be?" I questioned, "Where *would*
I be, Grandpa?" -- a small boy balanced on

his brittle knee. "Tell me, please," and then
he pondered those slim numerals again.
"That's a story for another time."
But the shot kept numbing; shattered by that thought
my own red life was leaking, drop by drop.

I TOUCHED THE HAND THAT SHOOK THE HAND OF LINCOLN

I touched the hand that shook
the hand of Lincoln ---
blackveined by then,
a liverspotted claw ---
"went, what they called later,
A.W.O.L." --- Grandpa said,
riding his highback rocker
"to see old honest Abe ---
the wind blew raw ---
and he stood on the back
of a train, talking of union ---
we all reached up
to greet him when he was through ---
Yessir, a good man,
straight and tall ---
he looked just like he looks
on stamps and pennies ---
except he wore
a stovepipe hat and shawl ---
but sad, boy, sad
and tired of war."
And Grandpa sat there
rocking back to Shiloh
and other gruesome
battles oozing gore ---
and he was sad and tired,
almost a hundred
(in spite of one lung
missing since the war)
wondering, maybe as I do,
who touched the hand
that once shook hands
with Lincoln
(who surely wondered, too)
what it was for.

UNDER THE ROSES

She lay there in the casket under sprays
of roses, stocks and gladioluses,
seeming to breathe although her eyes were closed
and her live lips had never glowed so pink.
Later I'd hear "When Allie passed away --- "
but that late date was still too soon to think.
Grandpa shuffled in while Rock of Ages
mourning from the organ shook the petals
and touched her hand and whispered "Daughter, daughter ... "
dark spots on the ribbons of his medals.
Two au nts rushed up and all that they could say
was "Papa, don't --- " "You know there is no death --- "
and it took all their Scientific strength
to hold him back before he kissed her face.

VETERANS

We had to take him out
in all his faded ribbons
to sit among the veterans
whose faces looked like webs.

The green lawn never ended
with flowers near the crosses ---
the Mayor spoke, and soldiers
fired saluting guns ---
flags waved as the band
thrilled us with its drums ---

high school majorettes
twirled and twirled batons
that glittered in the sun ---

and every year one less
folding chair was there
with hat and uniform ---

until above the bunting
Grandpa sat alone ---

but still the band's brass circles
blew Stars and Stripes Forever
for Shiloh and Bull Run ---
and still the lawn stretched on
with crosses crosses crosses
farther than Verdun.

EVERETT

Softly and often I heard tell of Everett,
my flawless cousin in the photograph,
almost haloed over his virgin curls,
with an eyelit mouthcurve tickling toward a laugh ---
so wellbred, so gentle, such a little man,
buttoned in velvet, tapered of hand.

His death was stark torture --- cancer that crawled
right through his mouth and all the way down
as he turned pale and bore it
with hardly a frown.
You saw he was going, my soft mother sighed ---
he tried not to show it. He smiled as he died.

Why was I mean then, toad-wordy and desperate,
finding things out and sneaking through weeds
behind backlot fences when a cousin like Everett
spoke phrases of pearl and did such good deeds?
And sometimes I thought I heard Everett say
"Perfection is easier once you're a memory."

WHAT SHE SAID

When a girl at the Farm Bureau dinner
dropping mayonnaise on her dress
jumped up and said oh Fuck,
not knowing what it meant
I liked its ripe fruit sound
and so repeated it ---
then felt a shouldertap
and when I turned around
a lady who'd gone red
said, "I don't know what that means
but know it isn't nice --- "
which hardly made good sense ---
a luscious word like that ---
the more I thought of it
the less it seemed to detach
from a tall branch and --- splat ---
make a gold sound on the ground ---
I didn't say it again
and it began to rot
like anything kept in.
Next time I heard it spat
out of some bully's mouth
it lay there grey as death,
and secret worms writhed out.

THE JOHNSON SMITH & COMPANY

Grown ups, no matter what we sent for
out of those pages promising so much ---
the sneezing powder and the squirting flower,
the gadget that could make a handshake buzz,
seldom were impressed, and if so, slightly,
reacted with indifference or disgust,
smiled for a minute, but not very brightly
at bloody thumbs and real looking guns ---
didn't believe it when we threw our voice,
though sometimes they were horribly convinced
that the turd wasn't rubber or the farting noise
came from Aunt Glennie instead of Johnson Smith
whose cruel catalog of tricks and toys
knew that boys always would be boys.

MISS HALE'S

Hoping improvement, my brother and I were enrolled
for lessons at Miss Hale's where in front of a mirror,
a full length oval showing us short with faults,
we practiced elocution for an hour ---
rewarded afterward with chocolate malts.

He went in first while I, in her horsehair parlor,
itchily fidgeted, as someone waiting for torture
hears in the next room a victim groan ---
wouldn't this kneepants childhood ever be over,
how many inches did it take to make a man?

In wrinkled rouge, she cherrily said, "You're next --- "
my finished brother sat where I had sat
and I went in beyond the door of beads
to give my reading to the ghastly class
as Miss Hale hovered backward ghosting my words.

Her little birdmouth seemed to be picking at seeds
or wide as a tiger's, spurted the blood from T's.
She ooed like eating lemons, clicked falseteeth.
I sighed out my singsong, waving my several hands,
wishing, I thought, if this was life, for death.

Action to words, she did a laughable dance
or sawed up the air with skinny braceleted gestures.
How many lightyears can an hour last?
How long until later in blunders' Wonderland?
Childhood was the time that never passed

in Miss Hale's inner chamber saying the speeches
and watching antiquity creak in a rigorous prance ---
and after that prisoner's hour being released
to knickers first and then to manly pants
and hearing of Miss Hale's death --- almost with grief.

LIKE ANY BOY

Like any boy, I needed something more
than self, and family of ambivalence,
an absolute, a god, I could adore ---
and lavished love on cats that through the fence
returned from fanged excursions missing fur
but purring as they were they weren't enough,
not worth obeisances with far-brought myrrh;
they lacked a certain magic star of proof.
Then one day playing, there in a dim lit manger,
I saw a new perfection at a teat,
and later lugged it home through streets of danger,
the very tenderness to ease my need ---
god spelled backwards, licking at me with pleasure,
a pup my father said I couldn't keep.

RUMBLE SEAT

We'd heard of what was done
by big kids in their teens ---
but under the moon what fun,
us in a rumble seat,

only eight or nine
and bumped through wind and light ---
whee! --- past WEISMANN'S DRUGS
and out toward the sea air night.

Melvin up in front
and Norval who got to drive,
laughing like silent films
while we shouted, bundled in back

and then through fields of beets
where the sugar factory chugged
Norval gave it the gun,
and holding on to our lives

we flew down the dip and up,
our stomachs gone like balloons
that drifted slowly down
and it almost seemed we would fly

over the curve where we stopped,
over the moon bright sea
as we tittered at what went on
in life's next rumble seat.

JUMP ROPE

Charlie Chaplin sat on a pin,
how many inches did it go in? ---
Kathy Cox chanted
and Lois Grant sneered,
turning the rope
in a viny backyard.

They were the curled first
girls I adored ---
willowy Kathy
and Lois's nose
reckless with freckles,
dresses with bows ---

giggling and jiggling
pink against leaves.
"Red hot peppers!"
and both of my loves
made me skip faster,
cracked at my feet

the arc of the clothesline,
widening grins ---
nastily Kathy
counted my leaps
and Lois, a Maenad
licking her lips,

flicking her hair back,
baring her teeth,
kept flashing her wrist
as the rope flew beneath ---
oh how I panted
and wanted to win

for if by a hundred
I hadn't missed
(they'd said looking wise
and I couldn't guess what)
they'd give me a prize
in the spidered garage.

TEARFUL OCCASIONS

Peroxide

They told me when I knocked that Kathy was taking a nap,
but liking them all, I ran in anyway
and right at the kitchen table there Kathy sat
among the Coxes next to pimpled Grace,
a slice of bread halfway to her mouth,
one of the cute striped kittens in her lap,
and under a pitcher poured by Marianne
Mrs. Cox above a sink of truth,
dripping peroxide from hair the color of butter ---
facing their surprise what could I do
except apologize, and big-eyed, stutter
I thought I'd j-just come in to say hello ---
then turned and ran, away from that sudden light
and sat on the curb of childhood and cried.

Perspective

When my fifth grade art teacher, Mrs. Temper, asked
"Whose is this?" holding my drawing up,
I raised my hand, small art enthusiast,
and told her it was the one that I had done.
"How could you have drawn it? Your name isn't on it!"
she said going red and her bangles crashing.
"And you can't handle perspective as well as that!"
I sat there watching her teeth that were large and flashing.
The chart of colors seemed to spin around.
But no one claimed my picture so I took it
off her desk, conscious of some great wrong,
seeing my name on the back where she'd overlooked it,
hearing the bell that ended the period sound
as the whole fifth grade blurred and flattened out.

Desperate Desmond

Desmond Petcalf, for no reason I could think of,
except that he was tougher and bigger than I was,
sprang out, at a party given by Marilyn Brinkerhoff,
from behind an oak tree and started to beat me up ---
quietly --- while I tried bravely not to cry
even when down on my back in the gravelly dust
far from the others, feeling his fist on my eye ---
he hit and hit me, mad with some kind of lust.
In the picture he's absent --- got up and sprinted away
when the kids squealed near with gay balloons on strings
and found me pale and bleeding where I lay
gulping the air and wondering about such things ---
I'm the short one next to Gloria Simms,
sobbing among the universal grins.

MARILYN'S FATHER

I remember him joking, the night that he did it,
at a church basement party, in an Uncle Sam suit ---
Mr. Samuel Delvin, Rotarian, elder,
well-liked, respectable --- Marilyn's father ---
grammar school princess, our cardboard show's star.

They found him next morning, headlessly slumping,
the rifle aslant in his brainsplattered car;
no note told the motive --- a half empty bottle;
we whispered at school --- "Marilyn's father --- "
and then we forgot, being lively and little,

until she came back, her hair curled as ever,
sadsmiling, pretty, but marred in some way
in our minds by the bloodblast that ended her father ---
innocent Marilyn, victim of tragedy,
the mystery suicide's deathspattered daughter.

JOSEPH HORWITZ

None of us thought of Joseph as a Jew ---
if he felt chosen, he never let us know ---
instead he was admired by a few
for the dark hint of being more mature.
In our spare sixth grade armpits nothing grew.

We'd heard before of Joseph and all those
others in a testament of gore ---
when Joseph's father, among cut-rate clothes,
was murdered in his Fourth Street dry goods store
all of us signed the sympathetic rose

printed on the card Miss Hurley brought.
We thought we saw the Mexican appear,
flashing a knife, and shuddered at the thought,
at every nightmare corner of our fear ---
death's elusive angel, still uncaught.

And Joseph did seem different from us
when he came back with black around his sleeve,
a sadder pupil adding up the sum,
though after he no longer had to grieve,
as good at soccer as he ever was

but even older, while we felt more bare
and higher pitched than ever, and who knew
if he had known some wife of Potiphar
stroking like Miss Hurley's glances through
the rich symbol of his lustrous hair.

ELEMENTARY EDUCATION

"Don't touch him --- stay away," the teacher warned us.
Our minute-before friend lay foaming on the ground,
his eyes rolled upward,
but why he should twitch like that no one informed us.
A line of blood came trickling out of his mouth.

We went away and whispered by the fence
"Larry's gone crazy." "I think he's going to die."
"How could it happen?"
"Joe, do you know why?"
Then the bell rang and all of us got into line,

craning to look back at Larry, the teacher kneeling
and signalling someone who'd driven up in a car ---
a woman whose bright beads swung as she ran --- his mother.
The bell rang again and all of marched on in,
straight and polite, though usually we pushed one another,

and told by rote the lessons we had learned ---
whether it snows in Timbuctoo
and when Rome burned.

LARRY WORTH

I found out he was all right
in every other way ---
sandy haired, blue eyed,
funny at times,
and he knew some words I didn't ---
he asked me over once
to whisper the words
and look at his pigeons
but he climbed up a tree
and started to shake
and when he fell
almost fell on me.
He was alive, though,
jerking and foaming
the way I'd seen him
that time at school
except this time
there was a lot more blood.
I screamed, "Mrs. Worth, Mrs. Worth!"
and she came out
and squatted beside him and said
"Oh my baby, my baby,
he's cracked open his head."
My mother wouldn't let me visit him
at St. Joseph's Hospital
or after he was better
go over there anymore
to play with the pigeons ---
she thought what he had
might be catching.

HECK QUINN

She didn't want me to play
with Heck Quinn, either ---
freckled, humorous,
my own Huck Finn ---
lizards in his pockets,
he knew where babies came from;
kitchen matches
flared from his thick thumb.

He might whistle for me
and I'd be out the window
off to some mischief,
sucking cigarettes ---
she didn't like it,
questioned like a policeman,
with all the right on her side,
"Where on earth have you been?"

But she couldn't stop me
slipping off like that,
flipping out my manhood,
pissing beside him ---
when he winked I winked back,
when he called I sneaked away
to desperate adventures
like those of Huck and Tom.

He stood there behind her,
grinning through the glass,
doing funny antics,
saying without saying
"Aw stick it up yer ass"
and how she would have screamed
and had Dad tan my hide
if she had ever dreamed
that boy I imagined.

BONES

None of them ever seemed to be in pain ---
Grandpa slipped and snapped his toothpick hip
but he was old and almost gone by then ---
a smile of Christian Science curved the lip
of nice Aunt Glennie, though she may have tossed
moaning the night before on beds of nails.
I never heard how Uncle Sol was lost ---
why bother youth with death's unpleasant tales?
To me their bright cheeks didn't look too pink ---
they were so careful not to cry or shake,
and to poke fun with one foot on the brink,
so sly with medicines and cleverly stoic,
I grew up thinking hearts and bones don't ache ---
much later felt they must have been heroic.

LIFE IN THE TOMB

In that grey tomb of a house
where everyone nibbled his words
so crumbs wouldn't drop, and an aunt's
hands clawed as thin as a bird's,
where even the dewiest flowers
shriveled and seemed to gasp,

a table of General Grant's,
beads in the doorway, the clock
forever a quarter past,
a love seat where love never sat
under the case of swords,
but only a huge fixed cat ---

the noise overhead --- so I heard ---
of footsteps and shuddering doors,
while Aunt Susan kept buttoned downstairs
among relics and rumors of wars,
was my great uncle John,
naked, chasing his nurse.

O PIONEERS!

I remember pretensions of an aunt and uncle,
lounge lizards in silk pajamas,
they tossed raw meat to their German shepherd
on a Newport floor,
lived in Chevy Chase and drove a Cord ---
the latest thing in sporty squareness then;
their house seemed like a white castle with archways and tile.

Thumbing through *The New Yorker*, I sat there
hearing tales of the Spanish American war,
in their beamed pale living room, bored ---
there was no one to play with, nothing to do;
they served Coca-Cola --- my mother said "They would,
                                                         of course" ---
and it was right up to date and very daring and new
when they got divorced.

TWO GRANDMOTHERS

Hannah

Contained in her frame like the oval cameo
pinned to her bosom pleated stiff and white
she didn't turn a hair to hear the radio
gloomily announce what Hitler did that time,
but kept on smiling, mother of my mother,
mother of hennaed aunts and my favorite uncle.

She smiled forever above the rosy heater,
under "The End of the Trail" --- a face I liked ---
deaf to Uncle Porter and Uncle Peter ---
china elephants in a tiny line
flanked her on one side and on the other
a gleaming abalone with CATALINA inscribed.

The plaster cracked, the flame-bulbed chandelier
swayed in the earthquake of nineteen-thirty-three ---
"Oh my goodness!" --- she tumbled to the floor ---
I thought she would have shivered to smithereens,
but when I picked her image from the dust
her kind grey eyes seemed smiling: Never fear.

Sarah

Her house of sliding doors smelled
the next day of last night's supper,
she shuffled in darkness under
a kitchen light at noon

wearing high button boots,
her hair in a bun,
gave springerles to grandsons,
ticking her tongue.

Swiss, Wisconsin farm born,
shapeless mother of ten,
Sarah, hard to remember
except as a smile that bent

eyeglassed, sitting on horsehair,
mending things that were thin
and nodding her grey agreement
in a shadow world of men.

The day they sealed her in
out at the edge of town
I saw my father crying,
I heard my grandfather moan

and wondered why they should miss her,
Grandma, who'd only gone
back to a dimmer kitchen
to leave the men alone.

TOPLESS

When men started wearing topless shorts at Newport,
my mother sniffed on the porch and cleared her throat
at naked navels and nipples and said they look better
in shirts --- here comes one now the old hairy goat.

Yet as the bellies paraded and pectorals passed ---
thank goodness at least some part of them was clothed! ---
and broad bare backs diminished down the walk,
redly rippling or jiggling tan as toast

she didn't go on into the house or home in a huff,
but sat there glued to the view with her silk legs crossed
and skirt at fashion's length below her knees
and watched --- you might almost have said with lust

if she hadn't snickered and sneered at what was disclosed
and smoothed down her skirt even farther and
                                        straightened her hat ---
not that she couldn't have ogled manhood at home
but she was too much of a right minded lady for that ---

though when as the waves of seasons went out and in
what seemed obscene no longer even looked stripped,
she sat quite calmly sunning out on the sand
half nude herself in the air where sweet sweat dripped.

MISS PLATT

I wonder if anyone missed Miss Platt,
    Milady's Vanity Barber,
who combed and snipped behind plate glass
    in the clean, slow years ago
in my treelined town now under the vast
    concrete and traffic flow,

if some, once clipped by her loving hand,
    neat sculptress of living hair
that fell like chips scattered around
    her pure white barber's chair,
noticed when beauty began to abound
    in parlors of noise and glare

that Miss Platt quietly wasn't there,
    and wondered where she had gone
with her little neck tissues and shining gear,
    and pinstripe aprons thrown
with such immaculate flourish for fear
    of soiling milady's gown.

Yes, I knew one once who followed her out
    to the country of bees and sun
where she practiced her art on any lout
    too lazy to ride into town ---
my mother, tardy at fashion, and late
    at forsaking a grace outgrown

loyally drove to sit at Miss Platt's
    whose scissors sang and sang on
as the meadowlark did in the rustling grass,
    and when her precisions were done
handed my mother a looking glass
    as if to a queen on a throne.

The town spread out, and Miss Platt again
    escaped into flower and arbor
far from the shoppes where new lotions shone
    and hair needed more than a barber,
and crowned by a glory Miss Platt couldn't trim,
    my mother followed still farther.

BIRCH STREET

I wish now I had listened
those Birch Street summer nights
to Uncle Peter's tales
of blizzards on frontiers,
his boyhood in St. Paul ---
but history was words
only heard at school.
"Now, listen, when you're old enough
you can write it all---"

anecdotes of Indians,
Sioux and Chippewas,
when as a rising shoe man
at some dim trading post
he'd swapped them out of moccasins
with pints of alcohol ---
a riverboat he'd worked on
sculpturing the foam ---
how young I was and bored,
trying to look interested,
staring at his wart.

But now that even that
modern time is gone ---
the watch chain on his vest
from which an Elk's tooth hung,
the fake gas-burning log,
the tasseled lamps, the footstools,
the white, glass-eyed bear rug ---

I wish I'd listened better
to the lesson of the past
as we sat there like a cover
by Rockwell on *The Post*,
while Uncle Peter tamped his briar
not so far away
from footpaths blazed by Daniel Boone
past Birch Street into space.

THE BANK OF ITALY

I used to go among the marble columns
that exploded acanthus when I was counter tall,
and wait there for my mother to deposit
checks through the bars, smiling, being small,
at the guard who winked at me from mustached heights.

It was like visiting a museum or a foreign country ---
the floor had wiggles of black in pinks and whites;
I stood there peering in wastebaskets richly green,
I craned my neck to admire the golden lights,
and went out as from a temple into the street.

But when Benito Mussolini began to be seen
in newsreels with Hitler, scaffolds xed out the shrine ---
we had to duck in under buckets and white capped workmen,
agile as monkeys, doing things to the sign,
and when they were finished, it didn't seem quite the same ---

the floor glowed marble as ever, pillars still held up the sky,
the braided guard stood winking by the door,
but over the front and on the slips I swiped
it said BANK OF AMERICA where before
ITALY'd been lettered, and A. Giannini
didn't glare down like the Mafia anymore.

GREEN ORCHARD

It was the ranch again, eleven cousins,
uncles in suits for once, aproned aunts ---
perspective a green orchard that stretched out
bobbing with fruit, buzzing with orange blossoms ---
at the top of the pumphouse, a metal windmill turned ---

but as in a dream, it wasn't like that ---
instead of teasing, Bud, the biggest bully,
smiled as when we sat
smiling in the picture on the lawn
and little Billy didn't tie cans to the cat ---

we all were caught at our best as the powder went off
under the tall palms in front of the scrollwork porch ---
you couldn't hear Aunt Edie's jealous sneering
"I saw a dress like that on the cheap side of New York."
My earthy uncles didn't hawk and snort

arguing money out by the emery wheel ---
it was, in fact, a selective work of art,
a cautious flashback of the raucous real
where the cock of lechery rutted far in the barn
and there was less to say than there was to feel.

As in Willa Cather's rural past
the steaming turkey had a clearer taste
everything looked better, a gleam was on the dirt,
Aunt Nettie never slapped her thigh to smirk
at pregnant meanings in a bulging waist ---

lean in our shirtsleeves, we all took turns
turning the sweetness of the salt packed churn,
and, while ideal uncles scooped it out,
altruistic aunts passed heaped-up bowls
to cousins scrubbed until nostalgia shone.

Section Two: WEST EIGHTEENTH

WEST EIGHTEENTH

I go down Main again ---
now children you will see
the street where I grew up,
a corner cedar tree,
a hedge, a slope of lawn,
the deodar next door
lightgreen in the sun ---

an apricot in back
I climbed blue summer days ---
against the grey garage
a canna lily blaze,
and all along the street
white trunked walnut trees
with silhouetted leaves.

I turn down West Eighteenth,
wider than it was ---
where are the trees, the lawns,
where have the porches gone,
of ferns and lemonades? ---
what cleats of progress came
to bulldoze lights and shades

and make my climbing days
a concrete parking lot? ---
but as we pass the place,
I feel what I forgot ---
those early loves and griefs ---
maybe it's just as well
time changes lives and streets.

BLACK ANECDOTE

Charlie's a nice nigger, isn't he, mama,
I asked my mother, at the age of three ---
and --- he won't hurt you, will he, mama? ---
the anecdote echoes --- *will he, will he?*

Polishing grins in the Baumgartner's Cadillac,
his overall stripes must have stopped at that ---
the episode echoes back and back ---
but he tipped, nevertheless, politeness' hat.

Later, my brother told --- "Charlie said
to call him a colored gentleman --- "
and uncles and aunts, when the bon mots were quoted,
tittered white pride at his black chagrin.

He was ebon all right, almost as black
as the Baumgartner's car, a part of the shine ---
clad from his cap to his boot tips in black ---
that drove furs and derbies clubward to dine.

Gardener, too, he knelt to the tulips,
digging pink palmed with his affable spade,
against his black forearm, bloodcups of tulips
in the ink green flutter of ginkgo tree shade,

and gleamed his hellos at us. "He knows his place --- "
gossiped my mother by bright blowing clothes
to pie-nice, flour-white Mrs. Lovett
and echoed again my "isn't" and "won't",

turning my friendliness into her doubt,
telling her bogeyman fear as my own ---
Charlie will get you if you don't watch out ---
as though he had sprung from my towhead fullgrown.

THE VEGETABLE MAN

Diffuse it through lenses of time,
the treed and bungalowed street,
a sprinkler on a lawn,
grass smells rising sweet ---
and slowly jingling along,
a truck with liftable sides ---
the roving vegetable man
followed by noisy kids.

Show him parked at the curb,
our mothers down the steps
from all the morning doors ---
some with their hair in nets ---
to test the melons and fruit,
to ask how much for the beans
while we in our bare feet
wait for what he will do ---

with an earring in one ear
and an impossible black mustache
that hat with its band of sweat ---
toss us a cherry or two,
like jewels in that light,
and wink one eye as black
as a ringleted Corsair's boot ---
as memory flickers him back.

NEIGHBORS

I dreamed of neighbors, housewives when a child
who smiled, who smelled of cookie dough and dimes.
They asked me in where words and sinks were piled
with warm things, chocolate up to the brims
of cups, of crusts, crisp in floured light.
They listened, amiable; they shrugged, they hugged
the boy I was, their cute especial pride,
and gave me tidbits, sweets and tarts of love.

But when I aging dreamed them, dreamed them late,
their doors were locked, the face they showed
peering through windows was a face of hate.
They kept me bolted in a winter cold,
a man dissenting they wouldn't let come in
the kitchens of their kindness ever again.

MRS. MARSDEN

Braided Mrs. Marsden, two doors down,
out of the bosom of her amplitude,
used to loose like great balloons of sound
arias over our neighborhood.

She sang so loud, at four I gave up naps,
but there were times when over the green lawns
her voice chased through the scales like butterflies
waltzing along.

A vaguely foreign lady faintly mustached,
she also had a husband and a dog
that yapped and snarled and clicked against the glass
windows of her song.

Once I saw her singing like a frog
puffed and wobbling big enough to burst
and wondered if a pin would hiss her thin;
I did my worst

to hate her like the gossips on the block
whispering guesses after she was gone ---
but in the trash behind the empty house
of what she'd done

I found a gift of postcards in a box ---
castles and flowers, statues of naked ladies,
and heard her voice, wherever beauty was,
cascading praise.

THEY

They came on canes under the feathery shadows
of red berried peppers in a blossomed tropic
on palmlined streets with sidewalk cracks where I
hopped and hoped and rolled on lawns of clover ---
when I was young the old went creaking by.

Splotched and crotchety and slow with troubled backs,
they shook their bird boned fists at any boy
who whistled past on skates and whee turned whirling
around the corner in pure boy joy ---
where I was young, old people came to die.

Beyond begonias, they dozed on rest home porches
in a blue shade, and only woke to cry
from wrinkled mouths, untwinkling, as I flew,
threats and curses at the noise of life ---
not being young was all they had to do.

I'm not there yet but find myself complaining,
like them sometimes, irked on this porch, too,
at loudnesses --- and almost want to shout
shut up, slow down, as laughter goes careening ---
like those old fogeys yelling at my youth.

MRS. SMALL

I don't know why I needed another mother
but ran with my hopes and hurts to Mrs. Small ---
an ample bosom toward which she would gather
my tears and smiles with a wide arm, pillow gentle ---
she had no son and I was the one instead
she liked as well as any boy not hers ---
in her house of comfort and of bulging bread,
a towhead brother to her auburn daughters
with whom I joked and talked as we played Hearts
out on their porch of fuchsias hour by hour
while Mrs. Small sat hemming pleated skirts
and brought cold lemonade, as sweet as sour,
but when dour Mr. Small scowled back from work,
I hightailed home, to wait for my only father.

MR. SMALL

When Mr. Small, in spite of medicinal whiskey,
had another attack and suddenly died,
I couldn't feel sad, but just as frisky,
whizzing my Yo-Yo, listened to Chandu ---
talking to God that night, I tried and tried
to pray the way good neighbors supposedly do
that he'd be handed a harp and robe of white,
but I was only eight and he was cruel ---
especially to boys who were always coming over
and laughing with his daughters on the porch,
or clicking pingpong, trampled down his clover,
and though he'd been a pillar of the church,
I hoped if heaven had a pearly gate
he'd ring and ring the bell and have to wait.

S. (OUR) M. (ILK) LOVETT

Tapping S. M. Lovett, Doc Clark said "Sun and rest --- "
When his heart didn't skip, his ulcers bled and bubbled,
and so, in a sheet like a toga, he shuffled out
to a little vined arbor he had, to be untroubled

which didn't escape our boy-bright backyard eyes ---
that thin pinched pale haired geezer who'd often yelled
"Get your damn dog off my lawn," or "Don't play here!"
white as a ghost, hoping to bask back health.

One at a time we climbed up the steep garage roof
to secretly peek in his leafy medical bower ---
and it might have gone on for weeks if Jim hadn't tittered
and almost slid off at the sight of such penile power.

Sour Milk seemed asleep, but there rose from the thick black
                                                          bush
where his corpselike torso joined his matchstick legs
an enormous member, pointing up like a tower,
veiny and pink, with balls as big as eggs.

He heard us and jumped as if shot at, winding the sheet,
and yelled and shook his fist and the sheet fell down ---
"Get out of here, you Hoodlums! I'll call the Police!"
by when, with too much to ponder, we were gone.

EBERSOLES' POTATO CHIPS

In a huge vat of grease
at the back of their house
they made potato chips ---
only a block away ---
white flakes in a writhe
flashed down and came up done

out of the tank of time ---
we watched and licked our lips,
a sample salted our day
and seasoned our talk with a tang
far in a balmy dream
of kind-faced enterprise.

And from that fragrant place
we ran out into the sun ---
Saddleback blue in a haze
rose at the end of our street.
Crack went the ball on the bat,
someone ran to base

under the walnut trees
where sun fell through the leaves
onto the dark green grass
like gold potato chips.
Crack and someone slid home
scraped by a manhole lid ---

what was a little blood
when the best team always won?
But the dank day finally came
when we limped out of the dream ---
Ebersoles' closed down,
sold to the faceless name

of a placeless corporation.
We stared down into the vat
empty of free creation ---
Ebersole told us to scat,
and out in the eerie street
no one went up to bat.

ELAINE FARQUHAR

The first few times we saw Elaine Farquhar
after they'd moved in, there she marched
with an armful of groceries, pushing a carriage
and still another baby on the way ---
"That must be --- tee hee hee --- some marriage"
was what we heard the hatted aunties say.

Pale Elaine plodding toward the store
seemed heavy evidence against the stork ---
not many months and there she went again
one of the kids pushing the other's cart,
the aunties tittering as we ran in,
"Isn't she expecting? Shame on him."

Next summer, two were tugging at her skirt,
one squalled in the buggy, and "My stars!"
wasn't she already getting fat?
"Not even Catholic, either," tutted the lips
as ice tea tinkled, and hat to hat
confessed that everyone had made some slips

but this was too much (we big eared pitchers heard)
especially on the wages that man earned.
And when she dragged past flat, with just four brats,
we couldn't figure it out --- although we tried ---
from the wistful riddle whispered by the aunts:
"They say the poor girl had to have them tied."

WARM DAYS

Warm days we saw her often on Eighteenth,
a platinum blonde who might have been an actress,
in filmy skirts, her face a mask ---
no one else's mother looked like that.
"Where's she going, Jim?" big Bill Blood asked,
but there were places only in the movies
where anybody went in picture hats.
"You shut up ---" little Jim would whine
as Bill Blood whistled, whanging the air with the bat
And whether or not she heard, she clicked along
breathtakingly swaying what she had behind.
"Ever seen her naked?" Bill Blood teased,
and Jim's pained face exploded into tears
and he ran after her and she stooped down
pushing the heated hair back from his ears.
And then swayed on, and we went on with our game,
forgetting about her, until, in an hour or so,
clicking, bouncing and jiggling, there she came ---
a woman we'd meet in a bar, some warm tomorrow.

*THE DAY THE GOVERNOR PLAYED BALL
WITH THE EIGHTEENTH STREET DODGERS*

That time when the Governor came
chauffeured in a Cadillac,
grey vested, pot bellied, bald,
to visit his stately sister
who lived on our walnut treed street,

we stopped our game and gaped
and the Governor smiled and waved
and said, "Boys, toss me the ball --- "
and one of us really did.
He went right out in the street,
and one of us flung him a mitt.
He even took off his coat
and rolled up his French cuffed sleeves,
then wound up like Dizzy Dean.
A feather could knock us over ---
we talked for weeks and weeks
at school and on lawns of clover
about how the Governor played
ball that afternoon ---
and it took us years and years
but it did gradually dawn
we too still stayed just kids
sliding into home.

UNDER THE EUCALYPTUS

Under the eucalyptus, I tell my children
when the Santa Ana wind blew on West Eighteenth
Baumgartner's writhing branches broke and fell ---
you couldn't plant much on that side of the house ---
his hungry trees sucked up our mineral.

He had a milkwhite maid and black chauffeur ---
lived in ease behind the medicine smell
of the torn pink bark and long pale flickering leaves ---
and one of his meanfaced grandsons shot my cat.
A boy within me kneels to the box and grieves

the friend found dead when I came home from school ---
the shadowing eucalyptus still sways overhead
raining its pods and odor of the past ---
my children drink and eat of what is spread
at a picnic miles and years from West Eighteenth

and listen to the scene that's vivid yet ---
the oblivious banker driven toward more wealth,
a small boy bending to a murdered cat
as the tall row of blowing eucalyptus
sends secret roots corrupting underneath.

HIROSHIMA

Smirking at ten, and thoughtless of the slaughter,
against bright cannas, I'm pictured with the dead
where diaphanous dragonflies curled to the fishpond water,
laying their random eggs as ripples spread,
a goldfish flashed to gulp, a moment after,
most of those unseen hopes as we went our ways,
Dad to his Sunday snooze, my lightedged mother
out of the burning sun to a twilit place.
Deep in dark, my brother developed the pictures,
I rode my bike or didn't go far to play
pingpong caught in the blaze with some dying neighbors
until it was time to come home to the grey array
of pictures that didn't show until much later
the Hiroshima of a summer day.

DR. EARL BLOOD, THE PAINLESS DENTIST

When Dr. Earl Blood died,
up and down our street
through low fog we heard a sound of sobbing ---
he who had filled and pulled so many teeth
no longer there
to stop our red gums' throbbing.

His daughter and his wife
went walking with their grief
arm in arm along the foggy street
under the crying twigs and dripping leaves,
scarves tied on heads
and high heels on their feet

that hammered vaguely on the grey concrete
like tiny tools tap-tapping deadened teeth
around the block
and back along the street ---
coats and scarves,
through mist, of two in shock.

Unfeeling of their grief, still we listened
and watched as the sun came out
and fog jewels glistened,
until they'd gone back in
to where he lay
painless in bed and quiet as after the din

of a turned off drill in an air of pure relief,
the jarring whirring over,
the numb face undercover
that had twice yearly breathed
close to ours
and far away as death.

FELICIA BEST
She gave scraps to stray cats, and fed the birds ---
that lady who'd moved in behind the Cox's ---
and told us wild kids with kindest words
not to throw rocks or put little toads in boxes.
She was a Quaker, which was some kind of religion
that didn't believe in make-up or colorful clothes ---
at least, pale in grey or brown, she didn't.
"How would thee feel if thee were one of those toads?"
We gobbled her cookies and thanked her and acted polite,
ma'amed her to her face, but behind her back
made fun of her ways, and if we had to fight
smashed one another with clods out of sight of her shack,
which one night, with her in it, went up in a blaze,
and none of us pulled wings off of flies --- for almost two days.

DR. FARSDALE

After the divorce, when Dr. Farsdale moved
into the colonial mansion on the corner,
he went right on healing ills and wounds
and kept the hedges and the lawns in order,

repainted everything until it shone
green shuttered and whitely antiseptic ---
one day we say him carry in his arms
out of the street, a bleeding epileptic ---

and he was always friendly and polite,
Samaritan to any neighborhood,
respectful and respected, but one night
showed a different side of doing good.

"His house," I overheard my mother phone
"was all lit up like Christmas in mid-June --- "
I'd noticed her at windows, looking out.
" --- that Filipino houseboy --- " she went on ---

"a wild party --- drunk, naked men ---
at least they could have pulled the drapes shut tight,"
behind the horror in her moral tone,
hennaed envy peeking through the blind.

HARRY CHIN, CHINESE HERBALIST

A joke, a front or what? ---
nobody ever went in
that house behind a palm
with a neat sign: HARRY CHIN,
CHINESE HERBALIST
two blocks down on Main.

Did he sell --- opium?
and, if so, to whom?
and was there really any
such inscrutable man? ---
padding down an alley
to sneak the groceries home.

A Chinese spy, a scholar ---
innocent refugee?
wearing a silken collar,
grinning "no speek-ee"? ---
a doughnut to a dollar
he wasn't like you and me.

Then lumber in a truck,
a mixer chugging cement ---
newness going up
(how did he pay for that?) ---
and on the bright addition,
in neon: THE GOLDEN FAN ---

and in tux and tie at the opening
under a searchlit sky
Harry Chin himself
and his Dragon Lady wife
greeting us all with menus
of lesser mystery.

THE SETH THOMAS

> "Beneath the satin finished mahogany, behind the genteel
> dial of the modern Seth Thomas lives that ideal of service ---
> the thing that never dies."
> — *Century Magazine*

It tapered, graceful, from its genteel dial
out to each side, that era's classic shape,
when no one hurried much, and all the while
it told gold hours that never were too late ---
flanked by a changelessness of dimpled smiles
of us and cousin graduates in frames ---
the redwood vase brought back down winding miles ---
the incense Buddha, the porcelain figurines.
Summer leaves moved mirrored in its face,
cold nights Dad lit real logs underneath
as it ticked on, neither slow nor fast,
a neat ideal on the mantelpiece,
which living in the satin finished past
looked at the time like something that would last.

GERMAN,

        we moved to time's repeated chime,
our ordered house a school of schedule,
and we grew up according to the rule,
three square meals --- at seven, twelve, and five.

We scooped and scraped and didn't waste a scrap;
our soon done dishes always sterilely steamed;
the centerpiece was wax --- fruit that gleamed
almost as if it once had stemmed from sap.

We clipped the hedge and edged the creeping grass,
drove on errands, mirrored neat and straight,
starting early, we were never late,
and we obeyed the laws, and knew our place ---

so strict at goodness, that it made us sad
when history later proved us to be mad.

ZELDA KEITH

After three attempts ---
gas --- aspirin --- and razor,
we knew where she went ---
saw the ambulance
to which they led her out
struggling, loud, unkempt ---
there wasn't any doubt.

Before that on our block
over the treeswayed lawns
we heard the curdling shout
"Bastard! Goddamn louse!"
and tried to guess the rest ---
"Oh it makes me sick!"
my peeking mother said.

We'd see them going places
sleek in tux and furs
with happy social faces ---
and next night even worse
words through curtain laces ---
a siren down the street,
policemen running in ---

then silence for a week
and then again her shriek ---
We turned, so we could hear,
"One Man's Family" down ---
and after that last time
in her half torn off gown,
wrapped and strapped in white

while he wept on the porch
holding both the kids ---
my perfect mother said
"Well it serves her right".
shutting up the blind
on every world but hers
the way you close a mind.

THIS IS KFI, LOS ANGELES

Through a golden cloth,
chosen by a knob,
vibrant on the air,
voices from a box!

We sat so carefully there
when listening was rare.

Amos 'n' Andy joked,
right there in the room
later the frost report
predicted whitest doom.

Fibber McGee and Molly
opened their closet door ---
Witch's Tales sent shivers
upward into our hair.

And then when I was ten
and tall as the radio then
Charlie McCarthy talked
sexily to some ---
we turned the dial and laughed
at Benny's violin.

With curlicues removed,
the box and our ears improved ---
green roundness like an eye
for better tuning in ---
the Metropolitan loosed
bubbles of shining sound.

Welles and Helen Hayes
like neighbors in those days
came and put on plays
at the end of the kitchen sink ---
the ear could almost see
a toothbrush turning pink
or FDR with Fala
chatting on a brink ---
and sometimes words escaped
that almost made us think.

JUNIOR

Every night his voice broadcasts the news,
coming into our kitchen like Gabriel Heatter
from the green tuning eye and the green cloth circle
on the old Zenith, and I tell the children
stories of Junior who was the kid nextdoor.

Capering on the sidewalk for attention,
he moved in when I was nine and he eleven.
I watched him from a tree as he turned a cartwheel,
and not to be outdone, hung down by my knees
to become his immediate rival, his magic
lantern show vying with my broomstick puppets,
his coal engine Lionel racing my streamliner.

Under the still leaves of summer we traded stamps ---
a whole set of U.S.'s for one of his Mozambiques.

Everything I had, his was better,
even his father's car, his mother's mixer ---
his red sore throat worse than my headcold pain.
No matter what cake or steak I ever ate
his richer dinner tasted twice as sweet.

If I started a newspaper, he too began one,
headlining slurs about the rag I ran.
As soon as he saw me busily clicking pictures
he'd come around with cameras in his hand.

For weeks we'd be friendly, for weeks we wouldn't speak ---
he'd glide by on his new English racer,
leaning into the wind and twirling in circles,
then I'd put on skates and spark around the block
and it wouldn't be long before he and his fabulous friends
were passing me up with wheels on their feet.

"Fred Allen's funnier." "No, Jack Benny is."
We'd argue hours, and it could end in blood,
wrestling on cement, locked breathless face to face.

Our mothers through the fence compared our grades.

But though his Samoyed snarled at my common terrier,
various forces worked to make us warier.
He trained off to college in the East

to become this newsvoice --- on another Zenith ---
warning of later weathers and worse dooms.

Hearing his poise, I often wonder whether
he ever thinks how foolish we once were,
one boy the other's envious competitor
when to be friends was what we wanted more.

Junior, if I could, I'd whistle our secret whistle
over Tom Sawyer's fence --- long torn down ---
and shake your hand and ask if you remember
those bright tin cans we tied across the air
trying to talk between our rival rooms ---
or that warm night we lay out on the lawn
blinking flashlight signals to the moon.

TIME IN THE EVENING

Time in the evening was a summer grass
we lay on after tag and hide-and-seek,
the darkness starring to a universe
over the chimneyed roofs along the street.
Junior said "That's Venus" --- where the leaves,
lightly lifting, let bright silver through ---
a pallid twinkling, like a light through sieves
spilled all the sky with widenings of view,

so even Norval, at the sudden arc
of phosphorescence sparking down the dome,
cried "Falling star!", and in that dark
we felt a closeness in the far-from-home.
The dippers tipped faint radiance above
the tops of cedar and the Main Street palms ---
we were too young to wonder whether love
or an indifferent force had fired those realms

and fit the earth in such a firmament,
but on the prickling lawn it seemed to us,
among the jasmine and the clover scent,
a curve of warmth that heard the cricket voice
and heard the train hoot elsewhere at the edge
of summer in our town of growing up
where for a time some evenings, brothers, friends,
lay under lightyears near enough to touch.

NERVOUS BREAKDOWN

Harriette Small came home with a nervous breakdown
crying he wants to do it all the time,
and I thought I was learning a lot by hanging around
pretending to be more interested in my Yo-yo ---
later with a washcloth on her head she lay in bed
and ate bright honey that gleamed in the shaded room
while I told her my plans for running away
and building a dog kennel ---
whether or not she was, she acted amused.

At last she got well enough to sit on the lawnswing
and we looked through hundreds of magazines
as the butterflies danced in the snapdragons
and the lawnsprinkler waved white wings.
She never told me anything about him
though I had the impression he was some kind of brute ---
so when he ducked in under the roses
and she ran to him crying, and kissed and kissed him
I couldn't have been more confused.

LITTLE BOBBY

There was a distant cousin I couldn't play with ---
handsome, beginning to sprout a dashing mustache ---
"We wouldn't dream of putting him in a home,"
I heard his mother I wasn't supposed to hear.
"He's all we've got, he's our little precious."
Whenever they visited, he'd stay out in the car.

I saw him glaring through the windowsmears,
holding up a one-armed teddy bear,
and making faces, though so tall and dark,
if older, he'd almost look like Robert Taylor.
"Such a little darling when he's good."
"No, we were afraid to have another."

"Whatever happened to that kid?" I asked later
when several times the parents came alone,
never smiling and seeming older and greyer.
"They had to have him locked up somewhere or other,"
my father said in a voice that cut to the bone.
"He took a knife and tried to kill his mother."

MAUD WINTERS' SWEDISH MASSAGE SALON

When Maud Winters' Swedish Massage Salon
moved in, the neighborhood slipped down a notch ---
that elongated son on a motorcycle,
the Wolfhound instead of a pooch.

In a gangster movie aura
everything looked black and white ---
men at the door, dark hats pulled down
and shirtfronts doubly bright.

Gin bottles gleamed in the ashcan,
the son roared home late at night,
a police car throbbed through the alley ---
something wasn't quite right.

We heard a slapslap as on rubber ---
Maud Winters plying her trade,
buttocks and belly of blubber
with an Edward G. Robinson face

steamed in imagination
and the son gunned off leaving tracks
of surmise toward some assignation
down at the Mexican shacks,

but he sped to his own beheading,
his life sliced by a truck.
And everyone saw two days later
when the funeral car drove up

Maud Winters and her daughter
on the steps of our wildest dreams,
dainty in black, and veiled
as beekeepers or mourning queens,

while the light seemed to pale around them
and the Wolfhound whined at the screen,
dabbing with delicate hands
at the face of anyone's grief.

MR. MUELLER

Dapperly mustached,
comparatively young,
he sold us Milky Ways,
slipped us bubble gum ---
among the Campbell's Soup
and rounds of Quaker Oats,
aproned, clipped with pencils,
joshed us with his jokes.

And he took pride in keeping
his store well stocked and neat,
cranked the awning down at eight
and creaked it up at six ---
delivered to our larger palms
legal cigarettes ---
not a name he didn't know
among the corn flakes stacks.

For years a tiny island
encroached by widened streets
and Safeways, Alpha Betas ---
he held out for the past,
greying in our service,
suffering heart attacks,
until he had to sell
graciousness at last.

EDDIE WEISMANN

He smiled among the EX-LAX,
swimcaps, candy bars,
still sold dollar watches,
peppermint in jars ---
and mixed a deft prescription ---
"Hope this makes her well.
And how's your father? Better? --- "
stood there in the smell
of lipstick, cough drops, drugs,
freshly printed magazines,
arsenic for slugs,
forever friendly, helpful ---

someone who in Rome
would have known which herb to use
on wounds of martyrdom ---
and smiled and patted shoulders,
handed back the film,
praising when it turned out clear,
with sympathy when blurred ---
and when he thinned and dwindled,
though slower at his work,
about the vulturous cancer
never moaned a word.

MR. VIRGO

He wobbled up and down
Main Street, underhat,
his bulldog on a chain ---

almost an albino,
enormously polite,
he smade small kewpie lips
at every passing lady ---
fearful of the sun,
only touched his brim ---
had an eye for beauty
that no eye had for him.

Where did he get those clothes? ---
circus tents for shirts,
belts for so much girth
through loops of hippo pants? ---
and did he have a giant's chair,
someone to spoon his wants,
poor huge too white man?

No one ever knew ---
or none we knew, at least ---
we never went inside the door
he palely panted through ---
there must have been a funeral ---
did anybody grieve
to see such burden lowered
where pity cannot reach?

71

THOSE VEACHES

Something was wrong with every one of those Veaches ---
the mother stuttered, the father lost his jobs,
Dorette swiped things from the five and ten,
no one at Jefferson got grades
as bad as Bob's ---

Rosalie had a baby but wasn't married,
Paul was in reform school, Jake in jail
or serving out a sentence more likely than not;
none of them bothered much
about little Dale

dragging his germy blanket, the snotnosed brat,
and sucking his thumb, his diaper halfway off,
while Grandma smoked a corncob on the porch
and who knew what young silken leg
mad Grandpa watched.

They were a genetic disaster like the Jukes
we later read about in Psych 1A ---
hare-lipped, knock-kneed, pigeon-toed, given to fits,
but a rich lady on Citrus Heights
adopted Dale,

had his lip fixed, sent him to private school ---
and at age twelve he preached a sermon in church,
choosing as his text "The Golden $Rule$",
with an angel tongue that made
stone pillars weep.

SCREAMING ON SEVENTEENTH

Screaming on Seventeenth ---
a street away from home
toward which I pumped my pedals ---
cop cars, ambulance
hurried to the scene ---

spiderwebs of glass,
a dented smoking hood ---
a bulge beneath a blanket,
a head in a pool of blood,
red beads that still rolled ---

I clutched my grocery bag
of cans and wrapped up meat,
among the crowd of watchers
leaned
from my seat ---

hoping it couldn't happen
to anyone but them ---
men in white with stretchers
lifting the victims in,
their wide eyes going dim ---

and turned away alive,
aware of a spreading spot
soaking through to my hand ---
feeling, as I balanced home,
the blood,
the blood of the Lamb.

NEXT DOOR

I was tossing a stick to my dog
and looking up, mid-laugh,
saw, glaring down from the leaves,
horror right next door ---
a man without a mouth
sawing branches off ---

I shuddered and turned away ---
what did he mean with his teeth?
was it a leer or a grin?

I tossed the stick again,
and looked back up at the man ---
easy in his jeans,
he stopped the saw mid-limb
to light a cigarette ---
chinless and lacking lips,
held it between his teeth
and started to saw again ---

I must have stared and stared,
forgetting the stick and the dog,
at so much innerness bared
and he must have been aware
of what I was gawking at ---

after the whoosh of the branch,
he flipped the cigarette
and gave me a friendly wave,
his strong arm glinting haired,
perfectly muscled and veined;

less hideous after that,
he let the smoke stream out
from the face he might have had.

THE SYMBOL

"sounding brass, or a tinkling cymbal"

It didn't tinkle --- with a brassy clang
sounding through the house announced
the Fuller Brush man or whoever rang ---
the doorchime I had made in shop at school,
polished and finished good enough to hang ---

two brass cylinders of different lengths,
and at the top, hiding the coiled works,
a kind of shield with an Indian symbol
I'd outlined, pounding, so it looked embossed ---
my one success at art that had a use.

Even my brother couldn't find a fault;
aunts and uncles nodded at my talent ---
it rang and rang, heralding the halt
who came to beg, the man who brought
the dog back that dark evening he was lost.

It would have blended in as time chimed too,
my brass accomplishment have been forgot
except the innocent symbol seemed to move
outward as if detached from bells of light
and billow blackly in our living room;

stamped on a flag that slanted somewhere foreign
and followed by a stomping swarm of troops,
the swastika of those who were finally dupes
could never again be seen to mean good luck ---
at doors not ours the hour of doom had struck.

THE TIMES

Crimson evenings, thudding at our door,
as a whistling boy on a bike whizzed it there,
The Times brought late news of death and horror ---
Dillinger finally killed, the rise of Hitler ---
misjudged, it sometimes broke a prized hydrangea
or decayed for weeks in a tree
in the too high air.

But almost always, spread before a chair,
the front page screaming RUMANIA; FDR,
someone behind it reading each new scare
or maybe only the sports or business part,
The Times, among our bric-a-brac,
hung like a huge fake moth
on a waxen flower.

It clung there monstrous in the turned on light,
politically conservative, lying about war,
the humorless funnies on a page inside,
even the simplest facts not printed right,
less truth than travesty, most of it a bore,
a grave mistake,
like much of our decor.

AUNT LUCY

"By 1941 we'll be at war . . . "
so my Aunt Lucy, who believed in tea leaves
and weighty messages from scales at Kresses,
told us one evening on West Eighteenth ---
she'd given up phrenology and joined
a secret group divining from the stars
and dates of birth the truth about tomorrow.

"But you won't go, oh no, you won't, my dear --- "
and would have fanned with wrinkles when she smiled
except a frequent mud mask kept her clear.
"You are a genius, you are artistic,
you will rid men of many misconceptions ---
pictures in the paper, and finally --- fame."

Once she would have read it in a name
or analyzed a palm to find which year ---
gone to a gypsy, laid out Tarot cards,
wary of the Hanged Man, hoping for The Lover,
or in a mystic mansions, clutching hands,
have waited for uncle Fred to eerily hover ---
now she only looked at astral charts
for whatever it was she needed to discover.

And it was fun, though some of the relatives thought
this necromancy Communist-inspired ---
"Lucy, if you don't watch out, you'll be shot."
But she went right on, seeming to be wired,
when dire predictions happened, directly to God.

By then, however, she'd seen surer signs ---
her neck began to wreck, a jowl or two had veered ---
she went away somewhere and then sent out
Christmas cards from Lyle and Lucy Scott ---
a new man on her arm, her chinline sharply sutured,
far from the future, when she next appeared.

PAST TEN O'CLOCK

"People are not going
To dream of baboons and periwinkles"

—Wallace Stevens

I walk along West Eighteenth
as clear as it was then,
the lawns stretch square and green,
the periwinkles glow.
Junior's oiling his bike,
turning and turning the chain ---
he tells me Amelia Earhart
went down with her plane.

I whistle up my walk,
open the mailbox ---
a letter from Edwin Roth! ---
Mom bakes apple pie.
Dad comes home from the ranch.
Norval's lathing a table leg
in a whirling mist of sawdust.
"God thank Thee for this food.
Amen."
We listen to Major Bowes.
I conjugate my French,
thumb through the latest *Life*,
and when the clock chimes ten,

take off my baggy clothes
and neatly hang them up,
get into yellow pajamas
that do have blue rings ---
and after I go to sleep
dream of a mad baboon
flying out of the night
and scream and scream and scream.

Section Three: COMING HOME FROM THE MOVIES

REWRITE

I have been busy rewriting the scenario ---
my life wasn't terrible enough ---
born in the twenties, I never heard them roar,
and though I lived during the depression, the hungry wolf
                                        slunk off
somewhere else whenever I opened our door.

My mother and father were nice repressed people ---
he wouldn't speak to her for a week when she came home
                                      with bobbed hair,
but mostly they smiled united, as in a family feature ---
hardly the right characters for a picture of despair,
and visibly, at least, not very sexy either.

But emphasis is easy --- I can make out of my brother
a teenage Cain banging me black and blue ---
that time dividing the money when it didn't come out even
and instead of flipping the penny he chopped it in two,
I can turn into some Bergmanesque sequence in which he's
                                      dramatically driven,
the girl next door can be made up more than she was,
they won't sing "On the Isle of Capri" at the piano or play
                                      parcheesi,
but later lights will flicker on backs and shoulders of lust ---
locations can be selected to look more sleazy,
and whenever necessary, fake fronts nailed up.

I'll add, as though I didn't know any, drug addicts and drunks,
a stone age sheriff, a crooked lawyer, a high-minded judge,
put on the ill-lit corners of night pimply young punks ---
no one will show delight in popcorn and fudge
whether or not they did, or thought, that palmy once,

believing the worst was only being foolish ---
nothing happened at home or possibly could
to change the script from the way it never was
when the world beyond us still looked brilliant and good,
and ended, like the movies, with ever afters of love.

THE JAZZ SINGER

You ain't heard nothin yet
said from the silent screen ---
an era ended then ---
Al Jolson on his knees,
in blackface, with white gloves,
biglipped "Mammy Mammy"
and we at the Orpheum
who'd bumped up to the city
over the rural roads
to hear the miracle
never could go home.

I sat O-eyed, all ears
on plush beside Aunt Lillie
listening to Vitaphone ---
no one would have to read
the words to me again ---
the pies would not be thrown
except with an audible whoosh ---
even that tramp I'd seen
finally would have to talk
as he comically twirled his cane
and did his funny walk.

Everything was sounding
louder when we went out ---
instead of squat brick arches
tall buildings loomed about ---
the little lanes had widened
into cloverleaves
and all our hearts were pounding
on microphonic sleeves
as Uncle Peter's Keystone Kop car
seemed to be roaring low
and streaking smog behind us
toward the speechless groves.

TOM MIX

A Stetsoned knight the screen made look much larger,
every Saturday he killed the badmen ---
arriving just in time on his dark charger
to save the girl and win the west again.

The bright dust billowed behind his quick clipclop,
the clapboard towns said BLACKSMITH and SALOON ---
when villains reached he always got the drop ---
he could have galloped straight up to the moon.

Which of us afterward wanted to be Indians? ---
only we knee-high halfpint little squirts
with one pathetic feather in our headbands
had to go barefoot and shiver without our shirts

while all the big boys of the neighborhood,
twice our size, found where we hid out,
and sure as Tom Mix of who was good or bad,
rode in with rubberguns and shot their brothers down.

THOSE TIMES WHEN RICHARD BARTHELMESS WENT UP

with a roaring squadron in a war I'd heard
one of my uncles would have had to be in
(if Grandpa hadn't lied before the Board) ---
and the dogfighting biplanes with cockpits looped and veered

I sat and watched the Jerrys leer through their goggles
and cleancut Richard going into a cloud
out of which he soon triumphantly soared
only to face, as the ratatats grew loud,
a German plane from which hot bullets poured ---

and meanwhile in the barracks someone scarved
who should have gone up but didn't was counting the whine
and increasing sound of the planes that were coming back,
and all of them sputtered and gunned and suspensefully
                                              landed
except for the flaming flimsiness Richard was in.

It was then, in those celluloid skies, as I went down
on the edge of my seat while black smoke spiraled up
and Richard's warm blood leaked like truth from my lip
before I scorched into glory, I was convinced
nothing nations could fight for was worth that trip.

OUR GANG

They talked fast out of the corners of their mouths,
showing in every film what tough guys are ---
those actors who played gangsters for my youth ---
Cagney strutting like a bantam cock,
Edward G. Robinson spitting his cigars ---

their tommyguns jumping, made getaways in cars
from where the guard slumped bleeding by the bank
or the old storekeeper with steel rimmed glasses askew
trickled blackly into his candybars ---
and they had blondes slinking in apartments,
with dresses like mercury, and blinking jewels.

How sweet the champagne glittered at its brims,
how crisp with power the stacks of money looked! ---
and when on two wheels in black sedans
they took the corners, pursued by shooting cops ---
though we'd been schooled to know how they would end ---
which of us kids, careening in our seats
away from goodness, wasn't with the crooks?

THOSE BUSBY BERKELEY MUSICALS

                                          were swell---
neon pianos with dancers on their lids,
stairways and sequins--- who could tell
from movie lavishments that we weren't rich? ---
some Americans went into a dance
on giant turning stages all the time
and wore such shimmering skirts and fancy pants,
though Main St. citizens couldn't spare a dime.
And that was what we really liked to see---
glittering fabulous sets and glamorous dames---
in "The Gold Diggers of 1933"
no one going hungry or in pain---
slick blondes hoofing it to beat the band
and everybody looking like a million.

MAE WEST

A velvet hourglass
with diamonds at her wrist
and ostrich feather hat---
too little yet for lust

(or so my mother thought
who let me go along)
I innocently sat
and watched her do him wrong---

her bow mouth like a kiss,
her body undulous---
young, I didn't miss
her pornographic bust
or hinged hip as she said
"Why don't you come up?"---

a mirrored bedroom flashed
though I was only ten
and not as yet abashed
by what she meant by love
and how much fun it was.

TARZAN

How often we wished that we were as wide as he---
the backyard jungles echoed with our calls ---
and we'd have jumped and swung from tree to tree
and swum with Jane in pools below the falls
if only all the blocks weren't so concrete,
if grinning Cheetah could have been a dog---
weren't those lions prowling along the street,
those gastrucks elephants that rumbled along?
With each new picture we were more convinced
our feet ran shoeless, we felt our biceps swell,
at our lithe loins we wore a scanty skin---
screaming from the treehouse--- who could tell?---
Jane might be in danger of her life,
and naked as we climbed, we'd have his knife.

GODIVA RIDDEN

We knew that Sally Rand took off her clothes---
no one ever did it in our town---
a few girls in bathing suits went by on floats
but that was art, a bareness rarely shown---
nudes at the library stayed behind a lock
and who would ask Miss Frost to let them out,
buttoned up to her throat against the shock
of having breasts, though there was some doubt.
Amazingly enough, however hidden,
the naked secret couldn't be well kept;
night after night, the town, Godiva ridden,
bobbed with thighs and bellies while we slept,
and every boy, starting at nine or ten,
dreaming the slippery truth, became a man.

AND GREENED MY TWELFTH, MOST VERDANT SUMMER

And greened my twelfth, most verdant summer---
joy without juice--- some girls began to be
visibly curved in places I stayed slimmer.
The written princess, to my shy inquiry,
deigned, from her horsy heights, no answer.
Through rainbow sprinklers, mailmen still might bring
the President's autograph, the sample cleanser,
the badge, the whistle and the magic ring.
Plump plums, pale apricots, hung hard and green,
the gentle tom came home with a bleeding ear,
Webster had never heard what some words mean,
my bothered father let me start the car.
A little later, through the rising heat,
plums and apricots dropped ripe and sweet.

THE ANNUNCIATION

If only it weren't there and life weren't either---
she knelt and prayed with her fanatic rag
against her father and against my father
who kept their slimy secrets in a bag---
and now I too began to have the sag
and darkly sprouted to her white disgust---
O wasn't there anyone in whom to trust?---
the meaning was enough to make her gag.
She dropped the Ivory soap into the tub
and turned away as wordless toward the door
as if a shining shell had shown a slug,
and never came to wash me anymore---
she'd heard the angel tell her of a son
and knew his hated coming would be soon.

THE FIRST TIME

The truth came out one afternoon in fall---
in sudden spurts, among the toothy pictures
of filmstars on the burlap clubhouse wall---
with painful joy, a juice past all conjectures
ejected out of that pink throbbing knob---
Garbo smiled blindly at my plight,
and Gable grinned cleft chinned above my shock---

how much more before I'd lose my life?
A good thing, though, I thought, it wasn't blood
and yet I wasn't sure just what it was.
I saw it soak into the old rag rug.
If I'd been dying, how could I stand up?
The stars gazed down, remote, immobile, grand.
Next time maybe I would try my hand.

AT THE BROADWAY

Savoring grape flavored Life Savers
while Greta Garbo suffered,
I sat in my seat at the Broadway
no longer short and fat,
but suddenly her Vronsky
or her dark Armand.
Next week Bette Davis,
Joan Crawford after that---
those were the tragic ladies
on whom my boyhood planned.

I would grow great for Greta,
give Joan and Bette a hand
once I was bigger than they were,
with a face sharpened and thinned
until it would fit in the picture,
and knowledge to help them out
if they should need some kind of saving
as more often than not they did
when I sat there sucking a sweetness,
a star eyed overweight kid.

How Greta cried at the Broadway,
and Bette raved or went blind
and Joan Cinderellaed sad and unwise
I don't know how many times---
And O I am changed but they haven't,
they suffer on channels tonight
while I watch their young faces patient with pain
and know I will never grow up
before Bette's beaten and poor Joan is tried
and Greta leaps under the train.

HIGH PLACES

I. Lost Horizon

The plane that crashed in Himalayan snows
took us to the heights of Hollywood
far from our burning slopes and freezing groves,
transported us to somewhere in the mind,
a Shangri-La where everyone felt good,
a place forever calm among the peaks,
potent as Geritol for aging blood---
no bone however old that ached and creaked.
Jane Wyatt ran there briefly in the nude
as, from a distance, Ronald Colman looked---
which was the scene we thought of when in bed
after the show we listened to the clock
ticking toward when we'd lose eternal youth
and , like Margo, shrivel with the truth.

II. Mutiny on the Bounty

That matinee the silver sea hissed high
and we were bound for elsewhere on the Bounty
under the ugly squint of Captain Bligh---
though it was filmed not far from Orange County
(in Catalina waters, we had heard)
we seemed to sail with Gable near Tahiti,
a desperate whiskery sweating crew on board---
the white sails bulged like pillows, blood believably
leaked from lashes on a naked back---
"Mistah Christian!" Charles Laughton sneered---
fed up at last, we made our sneak attack
and tossed the breadfruit and the captain out---
the overbearing father whom we feared---
and veered toward Paradise with a wild shout.

III. Wuthering Heights

Above the seats the heights were wuthering---
Heathcliff and Cathy in a tragic tale
showed us there were times and places other than
today in a sleepy palmtreed town like ours---
the phony cliffs and painted heath looked real,
a soapflake blizzard blew around the stars---

Lawrence Olivier with a deep appeal
and Merle Oberon whose glycerin tears
glittering down her cheeks could make us feel
we all had such a strangeness at the heart,
and instead of streets there might be moors
of high romance glimmering in the dark---
our low world, after the final reel,
transformed forever by a touch of art.

HOMEWORK

"Grand Central Station"
announced my radio,
and hissed arriving steam---
"Gigantic stage
on which are played
a thousand dramas daily---"

I did geometry
and between the angles
listened down the tracks---
the farthest I had been
was Santa Fe and back.

The disembodied voices
made love in my room,
I measured my circumferences,
wanting to be grown . . .
Not long after that
"First Nighter" came on,
magicked from the air
by Campana's Italian Balm---
I opened up my Latin
to an accusative case,
squeezed, as romance began,
a pimple on my face.

Would anything ever happen,
my adam's apple jut,
a mustache sprout on my voice?---
I faced the apricot
glimmering glorious
under a small town moon,

behind me--- AMO AMAS---
the open Latin book,
and whispering from a box
rich voices of the dream

THE CLEVER STUDIO

The men were always taking off their shirts
to show that they had muscles sprouting hair,
sometimes sweating, bloody, streaked with dirt
the clever studio had painted there;
you didn't have to guess what they were like---
skinny boys who'd got a little older
and finally put away their childish bikes
and grown a thicker neck and wider shoulder.
The women, though, had never been mere girls
with runny noses and as flat as us
or worn those bangs, and bows in grade school curls---
a thrilling thing had happened to their chests
and MGM kept the secret well
that such silk legs were ever good at baseball.

SUGAR AND SPICE

Sugar and spice, they said, but unconvinced,
and hot as Galileo for the truth,
I couldn't be content until I'd glimpsed,
like guessed at worlds seen close-up through a tube,
the thing itself, the curve of nakedness.
I had no sisters, and my only mother,
fearing my theory, locked her door to dress,
and so I gave a nickel to a brother---
not my own, but one with views to sell,
in secret, where a leaflight filtered through.
I swore that I would neither touch nor tell,
and saw his sister lifting as I grew
certain I was right, her skirt to show
the apple proof--- what every boy should know.

COMPLAINT

They came home early once and I didn't have time,
caught red handed, to pull my pants back on---
I had to tell them, wet and mussed with crime,
I'd taken them off because the day was warm;
not sure they believed my feeble alibi,
at least I'd fumbled, shrinking, into my shorts---
and felt a desperado forced to lie
to save my life, up before the courts.
If only Portnoy had been published then,
with news of liver, sox, and fucked brassieres,
how sadly innocent I would have seemed,
absolved from guilt and aches and needless fears
that I was going mad by being unique,
that soon I'd hear a ringing in my ears.

HEDY LAMARR

Some of the older boys had gone to L.A.
to see her in "Ecstacy", but they came home
saying it was a waste of half a buck---
"Shit, close-ups of her face was all they showed."
Then Hollywood brought her over and parted her hair
straight down the middle and made her mouth a bow
and when we went to view her in "Algiers"
with Charles Boyer, she kept on her clothes.
Her legs weren't bad, though there were skirts at school
with just as much to whistle at below---
not that we'd hoped for more from Hollywood movies---
but still no girl missed the innuendo
when we would leer, pimply and blase,
"Hey, Hedy, come wiz me to za Casbah."

LADY CHATTERLEY'S LOVER

John said "Lookit this" and took from a bag
only a book with a pale blue battered cover
and I said, "So what? Is this some kind of gag?"
Then he showed me the title: *Lady Chatterley's Lover*,
and opened it up and pointed his finger at words
which I'd never seen in print except on walls
and some not even there--- with a leer and a smirk
John said, "Wow, this book's really got balls!"
He let me read it, and parts I read more than once,
sometimes pressing it down to repress the result---
those two in the nude doing what I'd never done,
always feeling a penis some kind of fault---
and after I'd slipped the secret back to John
it was harder than ever not to be an adult.

ROBERT TAYLOR

Why wasn't I, I wondered, Robert Taylor,
wavy and dark with a cleft beard shadowed chin
instead of blond and bland, a teenage failure
shooting up so fast I became too thin,
a graceless no one in the mirror's frame---
Wheaties and Ovaltine couldn't help me out,
or shaving twice a month or thinking right;
I'd always lean there in the bedroom light
on West Eighteenth never to reach six feet
and it would always be the full moon night
of the high school dance when I didn't have a date---
sleeking my hair with reeking Vaseline
I whistled downtown to the Broadway where I kissed
Barbara and Joan with Robert Taylor's lips.

THE MARX BROTHERS

I never thought they were very funny---
Harpo with blond curls cavorting after girls,
Chico in that hat, Groucho's obscene cigar,
and those big bosomed women always indignant---
feathers flying everywhere, drinks spilled
down dresses--- they weren't the grand adventure
I was looking for---

the shimmering sets and bright sophistication
when Cary Grant, highball in hand, smoothtalked Jean Arthur---
and I preferred to Groucho's eyebrowed leer
the other feature, with songs by Deanna Durbin---
what boy would rather watch those foolish comics,
often losing their pants or falling in pools,
instead of a starlet

with bow lips, rippling hair and a nippled uplift---
I hadn't paid my quarter for Marxian antics;
when I went into the dark I wanted to see
Dorothy Lamour filling her sarong
or Carole Lombard's quivering chin at least---
a dream girl mad with love, with eyes of wonder
for the man I'd be.

BEYOND THE RAINBOW

Those kids we went to see---Mickey and Judy---
she a braided innocent in Oz
and he the lovable undersized Andy Hardy
troubled with girls in a town of never was---
suffered in those films but not a lot---
there was a rainbow somewhere over which
she found a land as flimsy as the plot
where she could sing, and trick the wicked witch---
if he should slip, his wise old dad the judge,
man-to-man, would cure his different thought---
and then they'd co-star, smiling and sawed off,
a little older and bolder but not very much---
on those bright screens they never could grow up
to be innumerably wed, or dead of drugs.

LOVE AFFAIR

It never was clear in that one with Irene Dunne
and Charles Boyer what the title meant---
they seemed to be only having innocent fun
and yet she *was* a woman and Boyer, French.
He took her to see his grandmother, Maria Ouspenskaya,
high up on the Riviera, wizened and wise
in her bougainvillea villa where violins kept playing
while she lacily smiled and gave them tea and advice.
Though often after the fade-outs you had the impression,
whenever the themesong "Wishing" began to get loud,
other things might happen, they acted like freshmen
on a first date who hadn't yet been around,
and nothing you saw on the screen could possibly prove
they ever really got down to making love.

THE HURRICANE

You never saw more unconvincing natives
than Jon Hall and Dorothy Lamour in flowered sarongs
and when they clinched on the grass in their wedding leis
the modest camera panned up to the palms.
On the plastic island against background shots
emotions and barometers kept rising,
but as usual in those tropic plots
nothing much looked real or surprising---

until the hurricane, and even though you knew
it all was done by wave machines and cuts
you couldn't help believing water blew
and crashed like that and drownings weren't just stunts---
you forgot it was only acting when Jon lashed
Dot to a tree, the storm-battered church was a set,
and the struggling people as the breakers smashed
had been paid to lean and twist and get so wet---

but when the wind calmed down and every star
(except C. Aubrey Smith, who often died)
had somehow escaped the water's roar and pour,
you were again in good old Hollywood---
where Raymond Massey could miraculously change
and let the lovers paddle away toward the sun,
he bare to the waist, she with no hair out of place,
as the studio orchestra triumphantly played their song.

DARK VICTORY

Bette was really great in that one---
even though George Brent looked like
a clothing store dummy, she batted
her eyes, sashayed around and lit one---
not much impressed when George tried
to get chummy, except underneath,
and I knew she was falling
for George with his fortyish bags
and pencil mustache--- I could tell
by the music--- but what made me feel
almost like crying
was, that though she had everything to live for---
a Park Ave. apartment
and plenty of clothes and cash, he found out,
being a doctor (which showed off
his sinewy arms in a flattering medical costume)
Bette was dying.

He had to saw open her skull
(offscreen of course)
and with Max Steiner's violins sighing, said
(while she wore over the shaved spot
a shining sequined cap
designed by Edith Head)
that though he'd cut out the tumor
he couldn't prevent a relapse.
Bette had changed, however--- no more
bitchy tantrums.

        They got married,
knowing it couldn't last,
and moved to one of those immaculate
New England sets, snatching,
among foreboding oboes and cellos,
every happiness
it was possible to snatch---
I felt sure that Warner Bros.
would find some way to cure her.

But then when she went blind
and bravely kissed George goodbye, and climbed,
alone, with the whole orchestra lamenting,
up to her bedroom,
I gave up hope that Dr. Kildare would ever get there,
and I was so shocked that they had let
Bette Davis die
I went out and bought more Life Savers
and stayed to see it twice.

COMING HOME FROM THE MOVIES

I walked home warily daring, my warm smoke guiltily blowing,
grown up almost that spring I turned fifteen---
coming home from the movies with the package in my pocket
and keeping forbiddenness cupped where it couldn't be seen,

thinking of stogies bobbing in the movies
as Bogie and Bette Davis did a scene,
their little coals glowing after the matchlight showing
his hand blackhaired and hers as bright as cream

In lilac scented evening, knowing where I was going,
I felt an oddness growing as I walked
out of the Broadway theatre where seeing was believing
and back to my nice home on a square lawned block---

what was my body doing, starting that funny feeling
down by the Lucky Strikes as I walked along---
could anyone tell my reeling head that in such a setting
this throbbing oblong problem didn't belong?

Who needed blatant bedrooms, nudes on a wide screen screwing,
or for a loosening view, the aid of pot?
when a puff was enough suggestion, in the old old world renewing,
of naked truth, whether youth was ready or not.

SOLO

Wasn't I big, backing out Dad's '38 Buick,
getting its feel, shifting it into high,
flipping the knob to dial in low sweet music
as the beach road poles began to go whipping by---
hadn't I grown since I first sat on a pillow
to see past the hood, and hardly could reach the gas---
that little guy--- and now this dangerous fellow
urging the horsepower on, lifting a match
to light up a Lucky, without Mom's shriek at my side:
"Oh my goodness, Harold, you're going too fast!"
They'd never catch me again now I could drive,
if they tried to follow I'd swerve down different roads.
I was the man at the wheel and they'd seen the last
of that mild boy above his bicycle spokes.

STARTING AT THIRTEEN,

                       I kept a diary---
all my secret plans--- friends who weren't friends---
a brother who beat me up until he got married---
that code of dots at many entries' ends . . .

and reading back I am that boy again
seeing too many movies, weeding the yard,
letting out into the dark the hidden man . . .

as it was poor Mom had enough men on her hands,
and I tried hard to be good, not let her know---
at least until later--- but while I wrote it down
and dutifully weeded and listened to the radio
(Mary Marlin, Oxydol's Own Ma Perkins, Dr. Kate)
seeds she didn't suspect were coming up from below . . .

a rain of words watered me
from the stormy books I was reading

and while I went soberly down the aisle
taking up the collection
what I was wondering was
if Christ ever had an erection . . .

"Sometimes I think I'm a misfit," I noted sadly,
November 10, 1939,
looking out over the dark roofs at bright Orion---
and would have lain down with any girl gladly . . .

my handwriting became more erratic,
my pages spotted with dots . . .
Margie Stoller got engaged to a mustached man with an Olds---
and then in late spring of nineteen forty
I finally found the poets.

PAST BEAN FIELDS

                                                          JESUS
                                                          A
                                                          V
                                                          E
                    neon-crossed with   S
past streets that thickened toward a towered center,
there was another world beyond our rim
which I was finally old enough to enter---

Olvera Street where brilliant chilies hung
and pale tortillas grew from darker hands,
Spring St. with its stores, Main St. with its bums---
a farther feeling as in foreign lands---

bean sprout banquets in old Chinatown,
or bloated groanings after smorgasbord---
museums, and the Planetarium---
the palmed metropolis had golden doored

palaces whose naked statues stood,
plaster-breasted, on initialed feet,
and carpets rich as Persia led you on
to latest lucid screenings of the dream---

maybe it wasn't Paris or New York,
but to a Winesburg boy almost as rare---
where Rachmaninoff played at the Hollywood Bowl
and Blue Boy burned among the urns of grandeur.

IN THOSE DAYS

In those days I was famous,
a real movie star
of my own home productions,
pictures in the paper---
many in my town said
that boy will go far.

The films were shot on week-ends,
winning praise and prizes,
acted out by friends,
shown at teas and meetings---
ambitious, I spent hours
gluing ends to ends.

Writer and director,
actor, cameraman,
the names I saw in theatres
blurred and turned to mine---
then dazzling spotlights faded---
I began to sense

poems and to write them---
movies seemed absurd
flimsy fantasies compared
with pulsings through a word---
I went from shadow brilliances
backward to a dim

archaic inner studio
to star there in my own
poems of identity
too secret for a screen ---
and that was how I came to be
nobody again.

ARS GRATIA ARTIS

Why I should dream years later of Margie Stoller
I don't know--- but in my dreams,
though I was forty-six and she sixteen,
an old time co-ed, she kissed my middle age
and I wiped her lipstick off like thick red cream,

confessing as I did, I'd always loved her---
those movies I made were only so we could kiss---
Margie, I was your Taylor, you my Garbo,
and even when I dreamed of you like this
saying you didn't mean to be so grown,

your breasts in bud when I was narrow chested---
behind this beard, I'm still that filmy boy
in a looped memory, forever there arrested,
repeating scene after scene's young pain and joy,
caught in an adolescence I detested,

I'd rather have been a Gable to your Loy---
but even if I should wake to find you by me
you'd sag there creamed and curlered at my side---
Margie, it's far far better you didn't try me---
in a dream by MGM, my perfect bride.

IT TOOK A LONG TIME

                                      to put away childish things,
there were so many and I kept a scrapbook---
then all the movies I shot
beginning at thirteen---
I found out I could do without the magic rings
and the map of Wheateenaville --- the Orphan Annie mug broke.
As soon as I started driving I thought I was grown up.

Home seemed to be smaller, farther from the center,
Venus hung like a silver tear in crimson evening---
everything looked different when you were almost six feet---
my big brother became my little brother---
I wondered where such perspectives would finally lead.
I didn't whizz my Yo-yo any longer
or send to Quaker Oats for cosmos seed,

wasn't even interested in getting the autograph
of Carole Lombard at the Broadway preview,
though still attended movies twice a week
and church on Sunday, closer than ever to Christ---
on the subject of loving your neighbor we really agreed---
philosophically, I pondered deeper on life,
unable to get excited as once about the Orange Parade.

And I was ready as any boy ever was,
sudsing my face on Saturday nights for a shave,
in spite of my father who said I only had fuzz,
to be a lover, but I missed the chance---
nothing but holding hands on date after date,
and never nearing, as I didn't dance,
in an okayed social embrace, the region of love.

That girl I finally went with had breasts all right
and at last exposed them saying I hope
you can take the artistic point of view---
trying to be Gauguin, I groped lower
until she began fading out like a 1940 movie
and with eyes as round as Little Orphan Annie's
said there are some things a gentleman doesn't do.

GONE WITH THE WIND

When *Gone With the Wind* came out
Dan Anderson told me
it was a sexy book,
recounted at noon hours
Scarlett O'Hara's doings
as we ate our bananas
under high school arches.

I was too busy to read it
but waited for the movie
and though some racy loves scenes
might have been cut out---
what a shock it was
when Rhett said right on the screen
"Frankly, my dear, I don't give a damn."

It must have cost
more than it really cost
to burn Atlanta
on David O. Selznick's lot---
and all those bandaged extras
and hundreds of guns and cannons---

I was glad
for every award it got---
"The best movie I've ever seen,"
I wrote in my diary, then dot dot dot

But when I took my children to see it
on one of its re-releases---
when movies were better than ever
and sex was less hush hush---
sitting there eating their popcorn
through childbirth and bleedings
in a fairytale plot,
they weren't so easily fooled
though brother still killed brother
and fire looked just as hot---

having been better schooled
by TV and Vietnam ,
they just didn't believe it
(knew Tara was only a front)
and all they said as the screen flamed red,
drinking their Cokes, was
"so what?"

WHEN I FINALLY WENT TO MGM

it was a lot like home---
not a lion on the lawn
and emptiness behind
the streets that only had facades,
with people on mere feet passing
where I'd had stars in mind.

A showboat on a river
ending at a bend,
a grass that could be lifted
on stages wired for sound---
the minarets of Oz
near Tarzan's rubber jungle
next to a cowboy town.

And some of it was painted
and some projected on---
it looked as if you touched it
the thinness would be gone
and nothing there but desert
as later screenings show---
illusion howling through a skull,

a film of how things seemed
before they carted orchards off
and battered down the scenes---
and less like fun and games,
vivid faces held too long
against the heat of time,
burning in their frames.

Section Four: HOLD IT

POP. BY 1940: 40,000

It wasn't as if there wasn't any culture---
in the S. Hurok series, Nelson Eddy sang,
and even Marian Anderson, which proved
we weren't white sheep hiding a bigot's fang,
and the Public Library carried a good selection---
everything from Beowulf to Lin Yutang.

Maybe a Louvre didn't reflect in our dryness,
but there were excellent prints that we could hang---
Bonheurs, Van Goghs, and Raphael Madonnas,
some real originals in homes on Citrus Heights:
Sacré Coeurs with the paint still almost wet;
and some of us had been on tours and flights
to Rome, Shanghai, and even to Tibet---

it wasn't as if we'd never been around---
only that we knew there was no place quite like
our BEST IN THE WEST!
SEE BOWER'S MUSEUM!
WATCH US GROW!
99 & 44/100ths percent
pure American town.

PASSING THROUGH

How beautiful the morning looked---
steam rising up from roofs,
green fields between the towns,
orchards of perfume---

He was Sam Compton's only son---
then came twenty-nine;
his father turned on the oven
and he had hopped a freight

meeting among hobos
ex-millionaires and poets
or ones who might have been
if only they wrote it down---

this width from sea to sea---
the swarm of stars--- that sun
on tracks toward infinity
clicking him back home.

He wondered about Zelda---
probably married by now ---
and Harriette Small, and Bev
and Athena Applewaite's cow . . .

How beautiful the town looked---
even its shanties did,
where he had had a darkskinned girl
when no more than a kid.

Should he jump off and walk
back into that life?---
put on a suit and get a job
and settle down with a wife?---

He leaned from the door toward Fourth Street
as the red lights flashed and clanged---
still there--- the four faced clock
on top of his father's bank

silvered by the morning---
the straight street rayed with dawn ---
and then sat back and lit a butt
through orchards stretching on,

remembering how it really was---
cruel, small, ingrown---
some day he would stop---
but not now--- not in this town.

VIVIAN

Balling the clay, she said, "Take off your clothes,"
but my cousin, Vivian, in spite of his name, all boy
(and eight years old)
stiffened his lip, made fists and said, "I won't!"
"Your mother," Miss Applewaite said, "promised you'd pose---
that's the way they did it in Greece and Rome---
and you're just right for Cupid---
that cute little nose."

He left her there in the light with her egg of clay
and ran home, starting to cry, through the fruit-heavy groves ---
"Mama, Mama, that old Athena May
told me, Mama, (gasping) to take off my clothes!"

O Vivian, Vivian, some day you'll understand
when you've been to New York as I have, when you're a man
sensitive as he was, maybe you'll be
an artist or poet and bring your works to me---
strong armed, loving as he,
dark-eyed and clever---
O God why did I ever
come back to this clodhopping town
of my martyred father?

It wasn't until Viv was over thirty---
his shirtbuttons stretched at his pot,
and a mind man-dirty,
that he added the tale to his stock of cocktail jokes,
whooping, there she was panting to pants me---
a making a gesture of zipping down his fly---
"Miss Applewaite,
may I pose for you
today?"

BELLE SMALL

She drew good trees at school ---
"An artist---" her teacher said,
and so her father bought her
nothing but the best

paper, arrays of brushes---
a spectrum in which to dab,
hired a man from the college
who showed her how to rub

charcoal for a shadow,
effects from melted crayons---
she won a ribbon at a fair---
she made such bright designs

her father called her Rosa Bonheur---
who'd done the horses' heads
straining manes and eyeballs
in a black frame in his den.

A life class in the city
finished art for her---
a man took off a bathrobe
and stood there perfectly bare

in African example
of the human form divine---
at which her fingers trembled
and couldn't draw a line.

DOC CLARK

Dr. Clark, paying faithful visits
to croup and flu and measles brought his bag
of medicines and stethoscope and jokes---
"Rub with Vicks, put on Musterole"---
poking ribs as he leaned down to listen,
looking deep inside as we ahed our throats

Or in his office, in a whiter coat,
while the big clock ticked, he heard vague symptoms---
"Nothing as good as air and exercise"---
and we went out, knowing we wouldn't die,
past plaster feet and bandages in rows
and finished ladies waiting for his lie.

How many times he had to get up at night,
how many babies squalled in his hands first,
whom he would save from sickness as they grew,
and if they suffered, help them not to cry---
how often was it his sad turn to soothe
the grieving who could only sob out: *"Why?"*

And he wasn't more than fifty four or five
when he came in clowning past the usual group
of ailing townsmen, calling them by name---
and leaning to wash his hands felt somewhat faint
and then while all the dying stayed alive,
dropped downward into the dark,
without complaint.

OSWALD SHRADER

What miles of excitement then---
the trolley showering sparks
all the way up Main
down Fourth--- lovers on larks,
ladies out to shop,
and I in my buttons and cap.

Now I sit on a porch
and watch the buses go,
an ancient dog at my feet,
the shining tracks below
covered by concrete,
the lines overhead gone, too,

and the bright red gold lettered car
on 101 saying EATS---
I remember reading in school
something by someone called Keats:
"A thing of beauty
is a joy forever---"

They say that he died young---
he didn't know how life tears
everything beautiful down.
My Martha these score years
rotting underground
drowned in a mother's tears

for our bright boy who was drowned,
pulled, one Fourth of July,
by a riptide out and out---
and clanged to the end of the line,
nothing but memory now,
my joy tugged under by time.

MRS. NICE AT THE TALKIES

Nothing was as good as it used to be
in the old days when she went to matinees
and Rudolph Valentino glowed on the screen---
now they had to have these newfangled talkies,
you had to hear what Janet Gaynor said
in a squeaky voice and even Laurel and Hardy
made noises when they got bumped on the head.

She didn't need to listen to Gloria Swanson
or Warner Baxter--- the world made sounds enough---
and she almost agreed with Mrs. Johnson
over the fence that all this modern stuff---
cars that whizzed so fast they made you dizzy---
was devil's work--- nothing the way it was
when she'd bumped over unpaved roads in the old tin lizzy

with Mr. Nice--- and oh!---
how dark and handsome he was then,
his hair as shining black as Valentino's
but parted in the middle and his hands
moving alive below the glimmering cuffs---
Buddy Rogers, pretty as you are
and holding Mary Brian or Billie Dove,
why do you blurt out everything and mar
the speechlessly flickering film
of remembered love?

GRANDMA FOLKSTON

It was beyond her
what got into girls today---
they didn't like to cook
and not one of John's three
would even darn a sock.

Alice with her book,
Mabel moping around---
she needed a good dose
of sulphur and molasses---

she and Clarissa May
looked like cheap floozies
the way they painted their faces.
Sally had spoiled them rotten.

You'd think to put up jam
meant you weren't quite right---
"Oh Grandma, why do that
when it's easier to buy?"
And off they went to the movies
with boys who were just as bad.

They all had things too soft,
not like the olden time---
that cabin in the woods
in northern Wisconsin---

oh she could close her eyes
and there they sat beside
the fire on winter nights,
birch logs crackling and snapping---

Father's beard red in the light,
Mother with needle and thread,
singing the good old songs,
in homespun they had made,
too tired
to dream they weren't happy.

ETTA JOHNSON

She'd stopped the clocks, they said,
the hour her husband died---
no one remembered when---
and said she still burned lamps
using kerosene
in that dark house with towers
behind an iron fence.

Huge guava trees produced
fruit in the wilderness
her garden had become
and squashed along the walk
under our speeding feet
until the city came
to buzz the branches off

while she stood shaking her fist
there on the scrollwork porch,
a bonnet from the past
in faded bombazine,
quoting her bearded God
and calling down His wrath
on a world that had gone mad.

ELMER SLATER

Injured in the First War,
a gold plate in his head,
he lived on a government pension
instead of being dead---
and drove around the ranches
with books, and charts he'd made.
"Look, I've traced your family back
as far as Catherine the Great"---
and tried to sell us lineage
to buy his wife a coat---
my uncles and my father
took it as a joke.

He'd stayed at the library late
inking the lines of blood---
"We're all children of Adam---"
they laughed him to his Ford.
He took up Watkins' Products,
sold soap with more success,
and later Mutual Funds---
"A smart way to invest."
We didn't care where we came from,
as Elmer Slater learned---
it was toward bright tomorrow
our ignorant faces turned.

MARIANNE COX

The Coxes chose Marianne to be a star---
her Lux complexion and her long black hair
made her stand out, and she had talent, too---
the way she twirled batons was something rare---
while prancing she'd be wheeling two at once
then toss them up and snatch them out of the air.

With a dancing pencil, she could copy faces
from *Silver Screen*, of Harlow, Cooper, Gable---
so clever her praising teacher gave her A's.
"That girl," beamed Mrs. Cox, "has got a soul"
and the whole Cox tribe saved dimes in those hard times
for a year so Marianne could reach her goal---

a trolley trip for a try at Hollywood.
She went with her grip, red lips, and new checked dress
and for two sad weeks sat around and stood
and breathed in that star dust air and smiled and wept,
but no one noticed, among the swarm that buzzed there,
how beautiful she was and how adept.

"They only hire relations and second-raters,"
Mrs. Cox cried, consoling when she came home---
"they're a no good bunch of liars, Jews and cheaters.
Never you mind, Marianne, your time will come"---
and she didn't mind too much, within six years,
wife, and mother of five, had grown past stardom.

DEACON ENNART

Deacon Ennart called movies "The Devil's Church,"
so pious that when he caught his daughter dancing
he locked her in a dark room for a week---
he built a pool where everyone swam in the nude,
but segregated, at specified times of day
(at certain hours of the naked truth
branches creaked as someone high up viewed).

The deacon rolled, at revivals down by the river,
jerked (almost off) and talked in tongues and prayed,
which was when one of his daughters, in a flivver
with a nextdoor reckless ranchboy, first got laid.
His only son also began as a bully,
but turned out kinder, finally, having married
a good woman who, too, hadn't been saved.

You might expect, with such a twisted sire,
children of violence or hopeless addicts at least,
but though there were few things about him to admire,
his eager progeny lived their lives in peace,
dropped church gradually, went to movies once a week,
and the old sinner, calling them Clark and Gary,
dandled satanic grandsons on his knee.

MARY MEECHUM

Her broad face freckle sprinkled,
big breasts that went
flop flop under a loose dress---
gone bad--- everyone said--- a beach rat---
she stayed down at that old house
alone all winter.

Her wrists were bandaged once
and both eyes black and blue
but even before she healed
she was lifting a glass again
in a dark beach bar on a stool---

she had a baby, born blind
and the pale, frail thing soon died---

not there after that
when families came down---
"Living with some bum---"
and finally "Mary Meechum?---
oh that one---
she swallowed a bottle of aspirin---
they didn't find her in time."

But I remembered her young,
not fat then, almost pretty,
sitting with me for hours
under a torn umbrella
as ripples lipped at the shore
and we leafed through sandy catalogs
from Sears and Monkey Ward.

Whenever we came to the bride's gowns
she looked out at the sea,
and her bitten nail on the fanciest veil, said
"Next June that will be me."

WIDOW WILLIS, THE CAT LADY

I'd rather know cats than people---
they don't make you so sad---
not one of mine isn't grateful
for being rescued and fed
fish heads by the plateful---
not like Amy and Fred.
How I slaved for those children,
gave them all that I had---
when diphtheria almost killed them,
sat night after night by their bed ---
scrimped for enough food to fill them,
and as soon as they could they said
"So long, Ma," never thinking
what it does to a stepmother's heart---
Fred--- he started drinking---
Amy--- she's not too smart---
making up, sashaying and winking---
twice married, the hard little tart---
but cats--- there's loyalty for you---
up in your lap for a pet---
pamper them, they adore you---
they don't run off and forget.

BUBBLES

That stately lady, Banker Burton's wife,
officiated as she was called to do
at proper parties, christenings of yachts,
appeared in print, low gowned and latest hatted,
below her patrician nose, a bow of dots.

And sometimes she'd be seen in city papers---
when still almost young among the rotogravure
visiting duchesses--- and one time in the box
of a turbaned Maharaja watching the races
at Santa Anita, dripping gems and fox.

But a good friend told me that once when she'd been drinking
with him and her teen-age son alone at home---
stemmed champagne while they drank bottled Cokes ---
she'd got up on a table and started dancing
and then she'd started taking off her clothes,

though stopped when she was down to bra and panties,
and led them to the attic where she showed
a secret trunk of antique joys and troubles---
sequined G-strings, gloves and ostrich fans
and a lifesize poster billing her as "Bubbles."

JOHNNY WALSH, CHECKERED CAB CO.

Not too much going on
in this two-taxi town---
I never delivered a baby
and nobody like in the movies
ever yelled "Follow that cab!"

But it isn't all nice old ladies
either, I'll tell you that---
one time Zelda Keith
gave me a twenty to take her
up to Citrus Heights.

Before I could open the door
there she was on the seat
putting a hand on my thigh
and saying she thought I was cute
and what a husband she had.

Jesus, what could I do
with two kids needing to eat---
and how do you say no,
for half what you make all week,
to anything easy as that?

A MAN FROM THE FREIGHT

A man who'd jumped off the freight,
after his canned bean dinner
walked through winter wet
to the Library next to the Elks Club
and leaned in the light and read---

the local and L.A. papers,
Karl Marx and *The Post*,
Democracy in America---
anything and everything
to stay in out of the cold.

But Miss Frost's eye was on
those who didn't belong---
noted the hunch of his shoulders,
the week's growth, the Goodwill coat.

She saw him crouching down
far back in the stacks
peering up--- or so it seemed---
a girl's legs on a ladder---
and swooping like a Harpie
said she'd call the police.

For tramps like him there were jails
and the gutter was good enough
for bums with grimy nails
and one brown and one argyle sock---
we had laws for outsiders,
on every door, a lock.

SLIM THE JANITOR

He came at closing time
to empty, sweep and mop
the messes they had left,
to polish and to swab
their desks, their floors, their halls
and shine their fingered knobs.

In men's rooms, scrubbed their words of wish,

in women's, blood smears off,
and sometimes in the office hush
prayed wrathfully to God---
Deliver me from evil.
Give me another job.

Into oildrum alley cans
he dropped their filthy scraps
and rats that writhed with maggots,
left too long in traps,
and coughed back up their hollow stairs
hallowed with his steps.

They found him hanging naked
one morning near the brooms,
eyes popped, long neck bent,
and written on the walls
of all their soon doomed rooms
his warning word: *Repent.*

THE SANTA ANA WIND

We all were someone else
struggling against that wind---
our hair stood up tingling,
sparks leaped from our hands---
the tiled stucco dazzled
as in sirocco lands.

Our underclothes those days
snapped against our skin---
tan leaves whirled and scraped
with a dry and papery din---
the eucalyptus air
burned like medicine.

Usually so discreet,
fiendish ladies ran
after their crazy hats
scampering down the street---
the preacher in his study
whispered blasphemies.

Loving mothers shrieked
I'll kill you you damn brats
and meekest children tied
cans to electric cats---

a demon had invaded us
to make us mean like that

or lie in silent lassitude
going dark with thoughts
of death and what's the use---
until the weird blast stopped
as if it had never blown--- and then
we seemed ourselves again.

MR. FOOTE, POSTMAN

A mad dog bit him once---
he'd had to have those shots---
relentless lugger otherwise
of gasbills to the box,
of invitations, ads,
and few importances---
letters with foreign stamps---
to Mrs. Liederkranz
the White King Soap third prize---
his post bag on a strap,
in uniform and cap,
sweating around the blocks
in summer, and in winter
with heavy coat and gloves---
and after tons of cards
scrawled with unmeant loves,
his hurting bunions done,
his calves untied of knots,
a man who might have walked
several times around the world
finally pensioned off---
to dream he flies on winged feet
with messages for gods.

JOSEPH AND MARY PILFORD

After her miscarriage
and the lamentable operation
they discovered the secret of marriage
others were slow to learn---
released from fears of pregnancy,
they could both be warm---

she sometimes his mother
stroking a crying son,
or a lover in a lather
riding his underman---
then, if he would rather,
she'd let him be the one

chasing her like a satyr,
pushing her back on the bed---
to them it didn't matter
which one took the lead---
before they were man and woman
they were friends in need,

adepts of the bedroom
doing whatever they could
to ease and please each other
and keep an even mood---
more like sister and brother,
irreproachably good,

going to church on Sunday
and singing the hymns to Him
who wasn't a god of thunder
but far from vengefully grim
when with so many ways for pleasure
created He them.

ROBERT FURNESS, DOCTOR OF DIVINITY

One time he climbed to the attic
with his Bible and his clipboard
to write his Sunday sermon
away from the screaming kids---
and saw in the nextdoor bedroom
Joseph and Mary Pilford
writhing in nakedness.

At four in the afternoon
practicing perversions
he never would have guessed---
figures out of Sodom
on a licentious bed---
Joe's head straying downward
to where her thighs were spread

and she--- he couldn't believe it---
one of the Ladies' Aid
doing *that* to her husband
and letting him do *that*
while sprinklers ticked along the lawns
and not far down the street
the ball clicked on the bat.

Such sinful and revolting
positions of the flesh---
Mary with nothing on
bending over for Joseph
right next to the manse---
What is this that thou hast done?
Clasping prayerful hands

he asked God to forgive---
and every Saturday after,
excusing himself from noise,
under the wasp nest rafter,
nailed to his personal cross,
listened for their laughter
and jealously watched their joys.

EDITH FURNESS, MINISTER'S WIFE

Spring exultances---
not like back East
where after months of white
green peeked subtly sweet---
but oh--- these salmon pink
sudden hibiscus bells, those
African purple jacarandas
transforming a street,
masses of mustard
jungling the lots---
and the smell of new mown lawns
mingled with stocks---
the fur armed garbage man
humming "Carmen"
as he lifted the can
and his sweatshirt went up
over his navel---
it was too much
for her Methodist blood.

TOUCHDOWN BROWN, DEPT. OF SANITATION

Muscle wasn't enough---
though he could have done much worse---
flunkie, boozer, factory hand,
driver of a hearse---

he liked to be out in the open---
soon got used to smells---
his good ear close to secrets
whispering garbage tells---

love notes, dried up condoms
behind a widow's house---
and once, a bloody foetus
wrapped in last week's news---

he didn't let the police know,
clanged the can by the gate---
God, he'd been in trouble
with girls in his own day---

a bristling football hero
they let have his way---
he whistled along the alley,
jumped down and shouldered away

a food smeared Motorola
that only needed a tube,
The Rover Boys Over the Ocean,
a hacksaw he could use.

RAMONA LOPEZ

Her dustcloth rolled in *The Times*,
she got off at her stop
and went to clean the houses---
sometimes out to shop
for busy leisure ladies
behind the lawns and blinds.

Neatness in an apron,
black hair tightly drawn,
pierced ears glinting crosses,
a smile for everyone---
so careful with their Haviland,
so spiteless--- not like some.

No husband and four children
(two with lighter skin)
racial tragedies unguessed
behind her even mood---
a brother in San Quentin,
a sister who'd gone bad.

And she was conscientious---
trinkets and extra dimes
she knew no one would miss
were the only spoils she slipped
with the cloth with which she'd polished,
cheerfully into *The Times*.

CLARENCE HOLMES, ATTORNEY AT LAW

Not many murders here---
civil cases, mostly,
more rapes than appear
ever on the books---
but I had a diller once---

nineteen-thirty-three
soon after the earthquake
had shaken everyone up---
Mrs. Edwin Mandrake
raped and cut in chunks.

The guy the state indicted
was one Ricardo Lopez,
a kid of twenty-one---
when they can't find anyone else
they nab some Mexican.

But I hired a detective
and got the evidence
of things that screwball'd done---
doctors, the whole history
proving Mandrake nuts.

As cool as Jack the Ripper
he himself had hacked her
then raced out to the Club
and drank from some blonde's slipper
while his wife's parts bled on the rug.

You think they went out and grabbed him?
That the case was open and shut?
That Ricardo wasn't gassed?
That the defense can ever rest
until justice is just?

CARLOTTA SEYRIG, PALM READINGS.
THE FUTURE PREDICTED.

They want me to conjure the future
so I've got a crystal ball
and I do some reading of hands,
having been taught by a gypsy---
my grandmother, Barbara Delance.

But the incense, the Woolworth earrings,
the dim lights--- all of that
is only the show they expect
when they drop in with their problems
mostly of money and sex
or what they should wear to the dance.

It's the mind I really believe in---
and I was born with the gift
though there are whole weeks
I have to admit
when all I draw is a blank---

but sometimes I feel those vibrations---
or call it whatever you please---
I pretend to see it in palms or the cards
or in the ball or the leaves---

but it's the gift I was born with
that showed me as plain as could be
the earthquake before it happened,
the tumbling chimneys and cracks---
and as if on the silver screen
Amanda Mandrake, who called me a fake
and prettily laughed when I warned her,
attacked by her husband, Edwin,
and cut into chunks
with an ax.

A FAITHFUL HUSBAND

Soon after their marriage
Jane Marx began to act odd---
heard God's voice over the radio

though no one had turned it on---
showed Jack her demon lover's
red bites on her neck---
milksop of a husband,
what did he expect?
And motherhood didn't help---
that bastard of a baby---
dirty diapers, bottles,
and the crying drove her crazy.
Jack came home one night
to find the baby strangled
but whether by her hand
or accidentally entangled
never could be proved.
At Norwalk after that
she wouldn't learn to weave,
never spoke, grew fat ---
for years he brought her flowers
in the women's violent ward
until she rammed herself with glass
and they couldn't stop the blood---
but Jack never remarried,
thin and bent and grey,
he drives out to the cemetary
every Memorial Day.

ABBY ARTHENOT, WAITRESS

Who says divorcees are gay?
After that it was over---
she had to go to work---
no husband, no lover.

She moved down from the city,
put the kids in school
and eight hours every day
grinning like a fool

praised the chicken salad
to Mrs. Bertha Gray,
told deaf old Mr. Potts
"Yes, it's fresh turkey."

In that white apron and cap
looked more like a lady's maid
than a doomed Karenina
whose tragic heart would break---

brushed the tips in her palm,
greeted new patrons, polite,
with screaming corns walked home,
tucked in the kids for the night---

where was it she'd heard
that saying that like a refrain
kept singing through her head
as she balanced plate after plate:
"They also serve
who only stand and wait"?

THE GOLFER

Quietly desperate, he kept coming home
to inlaws from the East in his favorite chair---
Grace's cousin or her Aunt Therese,
one or the other knitting an afghan there
and how they packed away the spuds and beef!

Or else they went out with Grace to some affair
or met the Old Dame coming in on the train
and he was left with a cold cut icebox supper---
and the ads to read--- in the middle of round three
they'd troop in gabbing and Grace would say "Kiss Mother."

He had to drive them down to look at the beach
or else to the Hollywood hills for a glimpse of the stars
as they yakked and yakked with Grace across the seat
shrilling into his ears their Oh my dears!
and at every jerk of the brake giving a leap.

And he couldn't have stood it--- Grace always so tired
and having those headaches, too, if while they snored
on Sunday mornings he hadn't got out his irons
and pretending to whistle off for some strokes at the course
parked the Ford near the house of a widow he knew
and they rolled and roared on her floor like coupling lions.

DAISY HEMINGWAY
DRESSMAKING & ALTERATIONS

A whirr and purr of her Singer---
a few pins whipped from her mouth
when the bride came for the fitting
and there was the luminous gown---
not easy to compete
with cheaper ready-mades
but with weddings and formals and hems
she almost eked enough
not to go on relief.

Chuckling at Charlie McCarthy,
Jack Benny and Fibber McGee,
watching Garbo and Davis
half price at the West End---
if not exactly happy
she didn't despair at least
until she met Jim Garvey
and he started coming around
early on Sunday mornings.

She'd had enough of men
but there he was calling her honey
and there she was letting him in,
taking his gifts and his money,
doing it on the floor,
in the tub and so many ways
she never dreamed it was done---
and at first only thinking him funny
when he tried the dresses on.

ANGEL RODRIGUEZ

A droll grostesquerie,
he had grown up emotions
in a 3'4" body---
waddling forward oddly,
treated as a toy---
the mascot of the team
though nothing like a boy.

"Hey, water here, Rodriguez --- "
the numbered giants called
and rumpled like a kid's
his hair while he went cold---

and on the daily street---
"Mama, look at that---"
"Shh, it's just a dwarf---"
he went wet with sweat,
hating to be a freak

but did a little dance
and cartwheeled down the walk
to show that he was lovable
even if sawed off

and usually he was gentle---
but mad, when teased too much,
screamed in both his languages
"Fuck you! Fuck! Fuck! Fuck!"
and thrust a hard arm upward
to prove him man enough.

MILE HIGH MILES

A big man in our town---
almost seven feet---
he would have been more pleased
with less to move around---
special shoes and shirts,
a giant bed for sleep---
oh you little squirts,
try not to grow up!
smoke to stunt your growth---
drink coffee by the quart---
in spite of so much size,
he was a gentle sort

and married in his time
a girl not quite five feet---
some tittering went on---
they walked along to winks,
seeming so mismatched,
the grand and the petite---
but when the genes were mixed
by chemistry of sex---
two daughters and two sons,
nature knowing best,
not a single one
higher than his chest.

K-O-R-E, THE VOICE OF THE CITRUS EMPIRE

Out of his adam's apple
a resonance evoked
someone broad and tall
and not the way he looked---

not many would have bothered, though,
listening at all
to such a slight unmanly man
unless beyond the dial

whenever they turned on
his Poets' Golden Hour
it wasn't Herbie Bond they saw
but Gable, Cooper, Power ---

at first only a fill-in
between important shows,
then after stacks of mail,
while strong men cleared their throats
and housewives leaked desire,

he became the one
announcing at all times
the failures of the crops,
the latest on the films,
with that voice of ice and fire.

GOLDEN GLOVES

He ate right, slept right, lived right,
training for Golden Gloves,
worked out every day
the way ballet improves
step by step by step---
cut bad once in L.A.,
still he kept it up.

And how his mother worried
about his ears and nose---
his father crowed with pride
wild in the smoky rows---
those shoulders under the lights,
what a left, what footwork---
the new world champ--- who knows?

But he got knocked for a loop
on his big night in Chicago---
never the same again---
paunchier and slow,
he sells sporting goods,
showing, in better moods,
punk kids the old one two.

ERNEST J. LICHT, PHYSICIAN & SURGEON

Gas-looped with indigestion,
he took another Tum,
stumbled down to breakfast---
coffee laced with gin---
and he was ready for the day:
removing someone's rectum,
making hospital rounds,
then in his Broadway office
tapping chests for sounds.

"Eat right or you'll die.
Cut down on cigarettes.
Walk instead of drive.
Take it easy--- rest---"
with a light in his cast eye
"Get a girl in your bed
if you want to stay alive."

But home beyond his lawns
behind Venetian blinds,
gobbled ice box scraps,
stale chocolates, gulped wines,
chainsmoked Lucky Strikes,
then rode the elevator
one floor to his crippled wife,
pecked her phthisic cheek
and lay awake till dawn.

TOBACCO. CANDY. MAGAZINES.

Here by the old West End---
not much of a theatre now---
I sell magazines,
tobacco, even rubbers
to regular customers,
and I've seen things in my time
you only see in the movies---

old Zachariah Friend
shot down in front of my eyes
by a hoodlum in '29---
those were desperate days---
and I took over the stand.
I keep a gun in the drawer
but it never happened again.
Mostly I sell kids candy
before the matinees,
but I keep some hot stuff handy---
Zip, Nude Views, and *Breeze.*
Wouldn't you be surprised
if I told you who comes by
like clockwork every month
without his backward collar
to buy the latest smut?

ARTHUR COUCHAY'S LADIES' APPAREL

I have to go to New York
to pick out the latest fashions
copied from Hollywood---
if it isn't sleeves it's décoletage---
whatever Crawford wore
when she'd risen from rags to riches.

The local ladies adore
knee lengths if they're the rage
and when Hepburn put on britches
I had to take the plane
to keep the ladies in stitches
that would make them look like men---
usually I take the train---

which is why I stay in this business,
those trips to mad Manhattan.

I suffer sometimes from dizziness
shut in this stuffy shop
but a good stiff breeze from the Hudson
invariably fixes me up---

sometimes champagne with a model
or a not too bad lady buyer---
and my wife's no worse off for that---
she's always the first one in town
who isn't old hat.

BESSIE'S BEAUTIE SHOPPE

They came in--- looking a fright---
grey again at the roots
and wanted the works--- the cut,
the rinse, the permanent wave
and she did what she could
to make their husbands believe
those bags were Claudette Colbert---

and also had to be
Bessie the listening ear,
their doctor and their priest.
She wasn't a gossip or pryer
but what she had to hear
before and after the dryer---
it was enough to curl your hair.

They were having hot flashes,
getting irregular
(well, and wasn't she?).
But what they were really afraid of
wasn't losing love
but losing their meal tickets---
they'd never worked a day

whereas she'd gone to school
and learned a useful profession
so she could keep a man
depression or no depression---
there were plenty of fish in the sea
hungry for sex and money
if Eddie should up and leave.

MILLIE'S MILLINERY

Some of the younger girls
don't care too much for hats---
I say going bare
on top is just a fad---
a hat sets off the face.

Where would my business be
if all the hennaed matrons
decided not to wear
hats to the Ebell Tea?
In spring you should see the store---

every lady in town
buying an Easter bonnet
with buckles, feathers, bows
or maybe sequins on it.
They almost come to blows

vying for the right one---
they'd go without a girdle,
they'd rather not wear clothes
than bow before their Christ without
the latest in chapeaus.

ZETA GOFF, CHIROPODIST

I tell them it's their shoes
that makes them Chinese wives---
vanity, thy name is woman!---
staggering on spikes,
squeezing in their toes---
as long as it's in fashion
any torture goes.

I cure them of their corns
pare their bunions off---
but they'll be back with more.
You won't catch Zeta Goff
playing their silly roles
or in anything but arch supports
and sensible rubber soles.

THE ARKANSAS TRAVELERS

Two sisters and two brothers
with bright eyes on the bigtime---
Jean with a nasal twang
sang "You Are My Sunshine"
while the chorus of the others
swayed and hummed along.

B.J.'s supple arm
pumped an accordion,
Esther plunked a banjo,
Billy strummed guitar.

They sang for us at Grandpa's,
they played at most church socials
sweetly harmonizing
tearful "Oh My Darling..."
and everyone applauded
and said how good they were
but Hollywood wouldn't listen
and Major Bowes said no.

And though they sounded fine
to us who liked that music
they weren't the Andrews Sisters---
too out of date and corny
for 1939---
so finally they disbanded---

Jean and Esther married,
B.J. got a job
trucking to San Francisco
and Billy for a while
(before he took to drink)
changed his hayseed style,
trying to groan like Bing.

MIKE ALLMAN

Rushing up, tugging his hat,
wet suggestive lips
parting on gleaming teeth
under a brush mustache---
everything he said
hinting glands beneath---
he talked to fluttered ladies
boldly in the street,
and masculinely ready
for poker and for beer,
his were just such stories
the boys liked best to hear,
of brothels in Granada
and knifings in Tangier.

He had a wife, four children---
a terror to them all---
so when he clutched his chest
on Main St. one hot noon---
sirened to St. Joseph's
in a dying swoon---
the nuns there had to stare
and so did Doc Magrew
to see beneath rough tweed
instead of a bulging jock
or boxer shorts at least---
pink silk underwear.

BERT PERKINS, STATION MASTER

Old puffers first--- then streamliners---
not all of them made the stop---
sometimes above the clicking,
faces going places
flickering like a movie
and rosebud vases shaking---

but sitting on his stool
patient at the station
in glasses that were ovals
he read adventure tales
and hardly ever traveled
the disappointing rails.

NUMBER PLEASE

You still can listen in
but it's not like the old times---
I've grown grey in this service,
plugging in the lines---
snatches of desperation,
lovie doves breathing their sighs,

sometimes one of those voices---
"Quick, get me the police---"
what face has she seen at the window,
what man's about to advance?
That I'll never know---
someone wants Paris, Kansas.

KARL BOWER, NURSERYMAN

Maybe you've seen on Citrus Heights
or the new fancy streets
some of the plants I've furnished---
birds of paradise,
oleanders, begonias,
every kind of rose---
strawhatted gardeners tending them,
mostly Japanese---
they have a way with flowers---
but in this tropic place
you don't need many tricks---
a little water and presto!---
geraniums from sticks---
maybe you've seen the trackside shacks
massed with bougainvilleas
no one takes much care of
and yet they bloom like weeds---
if only democracy flourished
as equally as these!

MRS. WRIGHT

I saw one of those schoolbooks---
it's a scandal that's what it is---
teaching we come from monkeys
when God created man
in the very image of Him.

I'm going to bring it up
next month before the Board---
think how those children's minds
will be forever scarred
by believing that atheist Darwin.

The Reverend Oral Dixon's
behind me a hundred percent---
those books have got to be changed
and the Genesis story put in---
what would the world be like

if we wasn't conceived in sin?
Call those Red lies science
and nothing'll be too lewd---
next they'll be teaching incest
by that Jew Sigmund Frood.

STATIONERY. CARDS. NOTIONS. BOOKS.

They sank what they'd saved up
and a small inheritance---
nailed shelves for a month,
at the opening, served coffee
among the attractive displays.

His wife in her handwoven skirt
and he convivial
with his pipe and English tweeds
tried to create an aura
of culture and good taste---
but except for a student or two
no one wanted Auden,
Toynbee or either James---
and the dusting they had to do!

Then after a half price sale
they did get rid of some books
and just in time not to fail
moved the rest to the back---

the greeting cards sold well
and so did the comic ceramics---
the cat with a cactus tail,
the miniature toilet ashtrays.

HELEN PAYNE, SPOTTER

What could you tell from spots?---
mud, blood, bits of food---
designs of oil dots,
tobacco geezers chewed---
dip cloth and get it off,
don't think, don't brood.

What leg in the cut of that?
or heart pumped in this shirt? ---
this one had a cat---
that one worked in dirt---
when the lover's knifeblade stabbed
how much did it hurt?

Don't dream, don't make it worse---
only a ketchup wound,
not like a matinee
where Tyrone Power swooned---
dab the thought away,
brush it as good as new,

give it to Tom for the mangle---
he'll smooth it out with steam
and go off in his Ford still single
with some other girl still green---
while tears drip like wax from a candle
and no one can rub you clean.

FAY PURVIS

Brightlipped under neon
for twenty a week and tips---
a car hop at Shorty's Malt Shop,
she watched the kids whirl in---

a shiny blouse, red slacks,
a pert little pillbox cap ---
who would have thought her thirty
or that she'd served time?---

Somewhere in Oklahoma
she had a teen age son,
somewhere in Arizona,
the grave of another one.

This time she'd be smarter---
if the medicine didn't work,
a certain Dr. Farsdale
she'd heard would do the trick ---

and after that, she'd move on
maybe up to Seattle---
God, these smartass kids---
listen to their prattle.

Tittering on heels
she wowed them with her hips---
"Hi guys, what'll it be?"---
anything for tips.

I. I. AUGEN, OPTOMETRIST

The vain ones are the worst
who never wore a lens---
not only handsome ladies,
men too resent my rims---
some of them up in their eighties
who should have better sense.

They all can see the E
even with half an eye---
it's the finer print
escapes the retina---
however much they squint
most of them can't decide

what's in front of their faces---
it's not their eyes that are bad,
some blindness of the mind
keeps them from seeing right
and I can't give them that
whatever glass I grind.

THE PROJECTIONIST

That little room got hot
but cool on the beaded screen
Astaire and Ginger Rogers
in sets like whipped cream
flew on down to Rio,
danced on a shining wing---
the ice pale face of Garbo
kept whispering "Armand---"

When the circle flicked in the corner
he clicked off the second machine---
and Cooper in "The Plainsman"
or Grant in "Gunga Din"
grinned their perfect teeth
without a missing frame---
the tears continued to drip
down Shirley Temple's cheeks.

Over and over and over
seven nights in a row---
Mae West teased W.C. Fields,
Grace Moore hit the note,
and at matinees the same
reel after unreal reel---
while he flipped magazines
shirtless in the heat.

But sometimes the big boss winked
"I'll need you after the show"---
slipped him some different cans
and bills in an envelope,
and for the boss's friends
with erections in the loge
he projected what our town and MGM
never brought to focus.

OTTO UHR, WATCH REPAIR

I look into the watch---
delicate balances---
this for a lady's wrist
and that strapped on a man---
a time for being kissed,
a time for lowering down.

I squint deep in the works---
the thin oil lasts and lasts,
the jewels let it turn
not too slow or fast,
if frost or fire should burn
it only tells how long.

The mainspring drives it on,
the handspring's tiny spiral
keeps it going right---
a wheel is in the wheel---
night day night day night---
it doesn't have to feel

the breaking of a heart,
the wrecking of a face.

"DUMMY" RANDALL

Only his mother felt
(who'd read Helen Keller)
what he might become---
she somehow eked the money
to send him north to school---

after education
he could clearly hear
the ignorant jeering "Dummy"
from lips that smiled before---
now snarled back screw you
with alphabetic hands---

one girl ventured close
not thinking him a man
and wrote "I like you John"
but when she heard the moan
his unused larynx made
ran away confused---

He soon left our town
to live again in Berkeley,
married one like him,
and after further courses
taught strangely quiet children
the language of the voiceless,

and, as he finally did,
to make the harder choices---
take silence as a gift
and those who are deaf and dumb
in subtler ways, forgive.

MARGO MARTINE, STUDIO OF THE DANCE

Ignore at your peril bodily rhythm.
The rhythm of body is all there is.
I studied for years in New York and Paris
and now I waste it on these bratty kids.
Smiles, all smiles, for their fat fannied mothers
dragging their endless Shirley Temples in---
still there have been one or two others

none of them Pavlova, not a Nijinski---
a girl once, though, who might have gone on,
a nymph in her leotards--- leopard and butterfly---
and I thought her serious--- then at sixteen
she eloped to Nevada with some pimpled boy
and wrote on a postcard "I see what you mean
by bodily rhythm. I'm dancing for joy!"

But the one I regret most is Leslie Aumaire ---
so proper and stiff at first--- what could I do
to loosen him up except here by the mirror
strip for him, strip him, let it all flow---
after which he got queerer and queerer.
You need checks and balances--- one mustn't go
too far too fast or you do lose control.

GEORGINA GORMAN, R.N.

Take a tip from that dancer
Isadora Duncan---
to express yourself is the answer
before you turn into nothing.

After all day at St. Joseph's
I need a change of scene---
that's why I'm studying dancing
with Margo Martine.

Those bodies, bleeding and sweating---
one patient--- my God---
exploded all over the ceiling---
one bed --- completely red.

I like to bend and bend
and whirl and almost fly---
not to think of the end,
only to move, to be.

CHEST 46", WAIST 32", BICEPS 18½"

He pasted pictures up
of nearly naked men
with giant chests and narrow waists
and bulges at the loin---
taped himself each day,
drank milk by the quart,
working out with barbells
all the way from York ---
felt the inches swell,
his pectorals define,
straining in the sun
won the competition
at Long Beach more than once---
an Atlas of the shoulder,
a back like Hercules'---
but he was getting older,
got looked at more by men
than curving girls he dreamed of---
modeled now and then,
got paid for making love,
though no one ever touched,
kissing that rippling skin
in beach hotel or studio,
the skinny kid within.

LURA O'LEARY

To the Chaparral Circle ladies---
in her reds of unconvention
with brilliant checkered sashes
and sometimes orange tams,
she might have come from Greenwich Village
or the left bank of élan.

They ohed her telegraphic poems---
messages tapped out
from a secret deep interior
of rapture and of doubt---
inquired about her father,
a corpse that still lived on.

And she was gay and glib
and often cryptic--- " . . . a shame,"
they said, "she never found a man."
"Oh, she's a nun--- art's martyr---
she doesn't need one--- who does,
who writes like that?"

And some contended,
when she drank the Lysol,
stumbling, sick at midnight, out of bed,
she only had intended, in the darkness,
to take a harmless
medicine instead.

IAN DI LANZO

Whistling deliverer of the evening paper
and happy little hummer in a tub---
at first a boy soprano--- not much later
whenever something needed to be sung---
The Vagabond King or Handel's "Messiah"---
one voice they'd ask would usually be Ian's.

The local teacher he did scales for
sent him on to lessons in the city---
"Don Giovanni" in the new tiled shower---
lucid notes that hovered high and pretty,
and then he developed darker, lower power,
could range from serious bass to falsetto ditty.

He might have been a Melchior or Pinza
but the lead's laryngitis in an L.A. show
gave him the applause that after which
he couldn't go back to waiting for tomorrow---
popular musicals made him comparatively rich---
what he'd really wanted,
no one had to know.

NANCY VAN DEUSEN

They gave her everything---
horse, clothes, private school,
ballet until she quit,
then lessons on the flute
(she said it marred her lip,
and locked the music up).

She sulked through half the Louvre
and couldn't be enticed
up the Acropolis---
the only thing she liked
on that expensive trip
was shuffleboard on ship.

She yawned whole operas through,
wouldn't pour the tea
as grateful daughters do---
though married the nice young man
they chose to run the store,
a joyless squarejawed bore

(she loved his red MG)---
in labor with the twins
screamed as if only she
had ever felt such pains---
watching her parents die
didn't move an eye---

inherited it all---
the house on Citrus Heights,
the tennis courts, the pool,
the store, the stocks, the rights
to lands of ore and oil---
and drank away the nights.

HENNA VINAL, BIRDWATCHER

An enormous storm shadow
from dinosaur time,
a marvelous large grace
like a Shakespeare line,

the high point of her life was seeing---
(or thinking she did) and she'd been
on Audubon tours around the world---
the nearly extinct California condor
gliding it seemed from Saddleback
with giant wings unfurled
to light on her star pine.

Elusive bird of happiness
right in her back yard---
it sat there looking down
like death or Satan himself.

Was it wish fulfillment
or had her eyes played tricks?
She was getting old, old
and almost extinct.
And though she wrote in excitedly
describing its size,
 the underwing white and bright orange head ---
most likely an inordinately large
turkey vulture
the Audubon Society said.

ADAM CRABTREE, BEEKEEPER

Hundreds stung me once---
and did I howl and swell---
but anything you love
is sure to hurt like hell
once in a while at least---
with people it's most of the time.
It's not so often with bees.

Some men have their wives,
with others it might be money.
I just keep my hives.
Thousands of little lives,
gallons of golden honey---
and are they ever bright,
even sometimes funny---

off on a blossom flight,
back to their house of wax---
so smart you wouldn't believe
unless you knew the facts---
dances, that's what they do,
and point, with their feet, wings and backs,
which way the nectar is---

if the old queen swarms or dies
they up and make a new one---
and after a couple of drones
flying after her screw one,
it's curtains for all those buggers.
Maybe you like it better
with regular fathers and mothers,

grandpas, uncles, aunts,
cousins, sisters, brothers---
well, good luck with your choice.
I've had enough of that.
I'd rather live in peace
with my pipe and my old fixed cat
and my perfect bees.

"RUBENS" JONES

At Laguna or Corona del Mar
he anchors down his easel
above the breezy sea,
strives there stroke by stroke
to better what he's done before
but always the canvas shows
the same green wave about to break
on beiges of the beach.

Rembrandt, Michelangelo---
Renoir--- he's seen their prints---
studied once in Mexico,
at Carmel, got some hints---

and he has visions---
not these seascapes
similar as gulls
but figures of Blakean prophecy
demoning whole walls---

the same wave arcing up,
the same brown rock midpoint,
and footprints on the sands of time
the sea is painting out.

AL BOOSTER, CHAMBER OF COMMERCE

Best damn town in the world!---
bigger every day!---
you must of seen our sign
out on 101---
by 1940: 40,000
and we'll make it, by gum!

New drives being put in
lined with fullgrown palms---
it costs a mint to transplant em
but class is what we want
and now the depression's eased up
you just watch our dust!

Have you been to the new museum?
Genuwine Spanish stuff.

Even an Indian mummy.
Mark my words--- you'll see---
five, ten years we'll be
an A-1 metropolis!

MAD MADY

Mad Mady went out at night to war on the suburbs,
armed with a bag of rocks and an irate crowbar---
broke windows in better homes, banged at cars
and stealthily slipped on back through her falling down fence.

Week after week, a secret one woman protest,
hidden by hedges until the police cruised past,
she struck again and again, chuckling when sirens
screamed toward the shattered mystery she'd left fast---

but one night Mady was caught *in flagrante delicto*---
someone had waited up behind plate glass---
and she stood there shocked with her rock in the sudden search-
                                                          lights,
a frail old whitehaired sweet Ma Perkins type---

"That odd little lady who lives back there in the orchard,
in that old house that's held together by vines---"
A deputy led her away, while she shouted handcuffed
"Git off my property, goldang it! This land's mine!"

REV. X. BURNS McDERMOTT

He was a not-bad well-met fellow---
in learned sermons, more human than divine---
there was a beaten road that we should follow,
no fiery pit for keeping us in line;
his hometown Christ--- nothing like Apollo---
would never have turned God's water into wine.

He told the old they'd rise in brighter raiment,
the young to go and work for better times
(the house on which he faithfully made payment
shone white and new on one of the latest Drives) ---
he joined the Rotary, fished, like Christ, with laymen;
if we should ask, advised our troubled lives---

baptized wailing babies, tied the knot,
saw the rose-cheeked dead down to their graves---
as he'd been paid to, shepherded his flock,
though it was seldom any of us strayed
from the straight and narrow path of least resistance,
going the way his good intentions paved.

HATTIE KING

Most people couldn't stand
the ugly end of things---
a bowel case--- drooling mother?---
they called in Hattie King,
went out to a movie
while she wiped bedsores clean---

with a bag of tidy ointments,
a smile in a nurse's cap,
came and mopped the vomit,
slipped the needed pan
under the wrinkled buttock
of what had been a man---

sat up with the dying,
never took a drink,
crooned tunes to stop their crying,
tried hard not to think,
fed spoons of warm pap, lying
they'd soon be in the pink.

But when she finally sickened
none came to minister---
her wrists and ankles thickened,
she lay there old and poor
gazing enraptured at the face
of Christ on a calendar.

FLOWER WORLD, L. P. BLOOM, PROP.
"Say It With Flowers"

For every occasion--- flowers---
yet none exactly local;
from a hothouse up in the city,
posies for the yokel---
brought daily in my truck
down to this blossomed Eden.

Cyclamens, gloxinia
in foiled pots for the sick---
for some old ended veteran
this wreath will do the trick---
I only change BON VOYAGE
to SYMPATHY quick as a wink.

Some dad you wouldn't suspect
comes in clearing his throat,
buzzes around the daisies,
asks how much per rose
and has a dozen sent---
velvet brilliances---

not to his wife, you bet---
well, that's the way it goes---
I furnish nice bouquets
for stiffs and Romeos,
sweets to those sweet yet,
thorns for the old crows.

PERCY TILG, MORTICIAN

Some are easier than others---
you take those accidents---
all my art's required
to give them back a face.
I had a war case once---
they shipped him home on ice---
what stitchery it took
to make him look half nice.
I wish the world could pass
sweetly in its sleep.

And you'd be surprised how death
erases lines so deep
they seem to have been carved there---
a touch of rouge, some lipstick
is all such clients need.
This one, for instance--- beautiful---
she's almost sixty-six.
When those tight strings of pain
untie they all relax,
in spite of rigor mortis.

Yes, we drain them first
and pump a liquid in---
composed of several chemicals,
not pure formaldehyde.
You do get used, in time,
to almost anything.
I had to go to school
to learn how it was done---
I think of it as sculpture,
and yes, I do take pride

in turning out a client
better than in life---
I hope when you've written your paper
on my art you'll think it over---
it doesn't appeal to many---
but you sometimes feel so good
having made a blessing
out of their having died---
and pardon my confessing,
but we could use young blood.

Section Five: CLASS PICTURES

ASKED BACK

Thirty years since we were gowned and capped
and then let loose into the unschooled world---
a card comes for reunion--- will I join
the class still grinning in its photographs
for cups of kindness and a few good laughs?

I certainly would like to, Harvey Potts---
to see your shock of redness streaking grey,
and more made up than in their rosy day
those high school nymphs now matronly and fat,
showing off they're not as old as that---

to view what wives and husbands which ones got,
to hear about the times and kids they've had
and prove that I have grown beyond their thought---
that skinny, inward boy too shy to date,
long-married, bearded, fatherly and broad.

Not being there, though, I can imagine it---
the waistlines, jowls and middleaging look,
the great success, the failed teacher's pet,
the one who caught the pass while pompoms shook,
remembering what he drinks not to forget---

those days when on the shoulders of the crowd
his grass-stained face rayed like a blessing saint's---
and hears the whiskey cheer, each year less loud.
The small town Whitmans wordless ever since.
The artists who have put away their paints.

That Spanish girl's voice so clear and proud
singing *The Vagabond King* as we sat enthralled---
what quiet cowlike *madre* is she now?---
the thoughtless meat who when their country called
went to be maimed and killed without a doubt,

in a free nation, that their lives were owed---
some who will be missing, some not missed---
and I among the absent as I was
when to be asked you had to join the dance---
that age when difference never had a chance.

MISS DANCEY

Not one boy ever told---
maybe it wasn't true---
"You know those arty women---
not much they won't do---
she probably draws them nude."

Though no one knew for sure
someone thought he saw
Miss Dancey's handmade earrings
glancing as her door
opened for Leslie Aumaire---

and then the way she bent
over Rick Wayne at school---
whom was the lipstick for,
the dark wild piled up hair,
unless for Ernie Rohr?

Unless the following year---
mansized at fifteen---
for Tony Myerbeer?---
nothing could be proved
except the School Board's fear---

they had to let her go---
she packed her artist's gear,
moved to Laguna Beach
and walked in the sea one night---
with so much left to teach.

LESLIE AUMAIRE

Few in my school understood Leslie Aumaire,
who plucked and penciled his eyebrows and dyed his hair
and dared the difference it takes to be a dancer---
in that night dark of my school not many cared
for any attempt at art if we didn't have to
and wouldn't go near the edge where his feet veered.

We booed him offstage that time he came dancing on
with a painted face, in a tight ridiculous costume,
after which I don't think he ever came back---
for us Swan Lake was someplace on the moon
and Leslie, if not a fairy, at least a freak---
who else would whirl with girls all afternoon

when bullshouldered helmeted heroes cleated the field?
I never found out what happened to Leslie Aumaire---
snickered from school, he may have left for the city
and danced into crime or into the limelight there
but few of us stopped to remember, and less to pity
a boy who practiced what we could only desire.

JESUS LOPEZ

He wanted to study Latin, himself a Latin
who couldn't recognize an English noun.
Everyone was kind--- we tried to help him---
even when he was funny, Miss Arnoldy didn't frown.

Most of our mothers, if they had seen him
with his long hair and crossed eye, besides being brown
and almost a moron, wouldn't have asked him in,
but we were democrats, who knew his heritage
and felt his right to grow up in our town.

We kept on being patient and whispered the answers---
he could have passed if he had only known
how to take advantage like some of his classmates
whose C's and B's and A's were not their own.

But finally he dropped out, and we might have wondered
at odd times, alone, what he was doing now,
but none of us ever crossed the fine line that divided
his night world from our dark daylight to find out.

BEN-HUR

On tests, we wrote amo amas amat
and then went home to find what Ben would do
to best Messala and to end the plot---
and sure enough, this persecuted Jew,
sold for a galley slave, and his kind mother
and innocent sister vengefully locked away,
proved himself better than any other,
made a comeback and won the thrilling race.
We learned the Latin endings of the case,
declined and conjugated, but in between,
read about this Palestinian boy
(as if Jack Armstrong triumphed in his place)
saved by Jesus so that he could be
Judah Ben-Hur, the All American goy.

MRS. GROOK

Whoever could compute
from tons of paperclips,
from red marks: *"Please see me!"*
from skylarks struggling through
the parenthetic lips
of Mrs. Gretchen Grook,

from rulers in her tone
measuring--- ta tum---
sublime soliloquies
and Wordsworth's daffodils
like astericks on stems---

program an IBM
with how much sinking dread
of boredom in the tome
opened with that hand
she wore the topaz on---

who in a sterile room
where bare statistics hum,
feeding the machine,
could fill out shrunken Keats
she bled to skin and bone

and unearth what was done
when dumpy in that dress
ruthless Mrs. Grook
shot nightingales down
with bullets in her look---
to come up with the sum
of those she turned away
from love of poetry
those chalkdust afternoons.

NORMA

Norma was a girl who had to shave,
only a final n from being a man---
what was she feeling as she stood so brave
beside her desk conjugating French,

her hair up over her ears and combed behind
as if a brother stood there in her place?---
did she also have a mannish mind
behind the tell-tale stubble of her face?

She had to walk alone, smoked cigarettes,
wore a shirt and tie and pants sometimes,
but didn't belong in male or female sets,
friendless as if appearances were crimes

instead of hormones--- O Megan Regan
sitting in the next row, curved, with curls,
you never knew how much you were mistaken
vivaing the difference between boys and girls.

MISS DARK

She sometimes cried in class---
Miss Melissa Dark---
leaving some girl in charge,
ran crying from the room.
We read what Shakespeare said---
"O swear not by the moon!"

And one was Romeo
and one the bawdy Nurse,

passages too purple
bowdlerized, of course.
We did our sophomore best
to understand the verse,

whispered now and then---
"She and Mr. Lutz
drove off after the game
with a basket and a blanket---
isn't that chain she wears
his name on an anklet?"

The circled orb changed monthly---
by summer we forgot,
though some of us were lovers
and some too timid yet---
September Miss Dark went on leave
and Mr. Lutz had left.

Later as a Mrs.
Someone she came back,
married and miscarried---
so rumor had the myth---
"Nervous breakdown." "Tragic love."
And then we read *Macbeth*.

DOLORES KNIGHT

The only thing she had, she gave quite freely---
at first in vacant houses and weed high lots,
and then on Citrus Heights when boys drove cars---
giggled at school, passed notes that were full of plots.

Her skinny lovers didn't really like her---
that sausage hair, those round, eye-doubling glasses,
but horny, they were eager enough to hike her
skirt up in the dark or after classes---

secretly smoking, laughed about their luck
and told the others--- "Hey, if you're hard up
ask Dolores--- boy does she like to fuck---"
licked sweetness from her overrunning cup,

and felt grown up, guffawing in lower octaves.
Dolores, however, wasn't entirely stupid,

and when she finally swelled, chose from her loves
the one who came closest to being wounded by Cupid---

Frank Beach, kinder than some, and more easily frightened;
they both dropped out, and after they were married,
the others felt a heavy burden lightened---
Adams no longer of the guilt she carried.

WORLD HISTORY

Listing boring wars,
pointing to the Rhine
(while we wrote notes and folded
paper aeroplanes)
Mr. Carver tried and tried
but never touched the mind---

Magna Charta, Ghent and Trent,
fourteen-ninety-two---
we studied heads ahead of us,
watched the clock of now---

Ferdinand in plumes
shot riding in his car
like some old flickering movie---
"Lafayette, we are here!"

Mr. Carver quoted dates
(none good as Saturday---
wow! what legs, what lips, what boobs!---
would June come, after May?)

He never reached the present---
endless time ran short---
we got our papers back,
droned our last report,

and thought that it was over,
irrelevant--- not new---
but Mr. Carver's deadly course
kept on coming true.

MR. BYRON JARVIS

He read us anti-war
plays in a various voice---
"Bury the Dead" by Irwin Shaw,
"da Capo" by Millay
until there seemed no choice---
when, if there came a day
of armaments and uniforms---
of what we'd have to say.

Mr. Byron Jarvis---
dapper, avant garde,
reading e. e. cummings'
humanistic word---
delivering the news of truth,
calling war a crime
when hero patriots could look,
in the light of peace, absurd.

Then papers boomed on porches
headlines like a storm---
NAZIS, BLACKSHIRTS, LIDICE---
and in that dark, no ray---
Mr. Jarvis signed up soon
to die in a dim campaign,
a brave fair weather pacifist
like many who were slain.

ÜBER ALLES

Onstage a Swastika
and good Old Glory, too---
a girl from Nazi Germany
explaining what was new,
plain, with braids,
in uniform,
an Aryan through and through---
(although she didn't mention
hatred of the Jew).

We listened to her spiel,
open minded--- older boys
with eyes that peeled
her nippled blouse
thought they saw her nude.

Wasn't she friendly,
healthy, blonde?---
a home room teacher praised
dedicated strength of youth,
accusing, as she did,
us of gum and crudity---

and no one dreamed that day
the girl who'd stood before us
proudly pure and straight
was a whore that some might screw
(when Nazism proved
as base as any bannered cause)
for a Hershey bar or two.

REX WISHNEVSKI

Oddball, screwball--- hey, Rex, where's his mama?---
always that briefcase with his lunch and music---
he played on stages of an inner drama
and didn't care which side was winning or losing.

Out of his window, Études, Polonaise,
as the bat whacked or the football whished its leather---
cocoons of sound shut in, rainy days,
unwound and flew through blue in brighter weather.

And he endured the scales of ridicule,
the noisy sameness of the practiced ways
boys have always had of baiting the fool---
"What does he do, jerk off while he plays?"

"Hey, Ludwig, are you in love with your piano?"
left for Juilliard later, dreaming still---
married, it was said, a black soprano---
conscripted into the army, wouldn't kill---

and some boys died, or went where life was leading
toward drink or small success or desperation---
but none, except Rex Wishnevski, that weird kid of their teasing,
became a name that's known throughout the nation.

PHYSICS

Supposedly doing experiments
that went over our heads
John kept making eyes
at Margie Stoller instead---
equations on the blackboard,
equipment looking like
coils in the castle
of Dr. Frankenstein.

Lilac outside the windows---
pines, the smell of grass---
and Margie Stoller's sweater
and Margie Stoller's face---
ions and electrodes
couldn't compete with those---
who wouldn't rather be
with her by a sea edge lace?

Somehow we got the workbook done
and barely made our C's---
but even when John asked her
she already had a date---
somewhere it was never spring,
somewhere even then
pondering $E=mc_2$
bent dedicated men.

MR. MUSIC

Flute, oboe, clarinet,
harp, bass, glockenspiel---
hardly an instrument
he hadn't taught those kids
(or tried his patient best)
when all he wanted to do
was play the violin---
wept when Heifetz pulled
Beethoven, Mendelssohn,
like rainbow silk from the strings,

thinking, clutching his seat,
it could have been me---
tapping his baton
shouted "Sharp, not flat!"
(A spitball from the drum).
Squeaked scales when only seven---
never had much fun---
four years in Chicago,
two and a half in London---
gulped aspirin for what?---
a high school production
of *"The Vagabond King."*

RITA RUBIO

A voice of soaring wing
edged as if with light---
she sang in *"The Vagabond King,"*
warbler of delight,
pitched perfect--- the painted stones
looked rounder when her voice
warmed them with those tones
fluttered from sunniness
and dazzled in duets
with tenor, baritone---
it was her night of nights,
sheened where the spotlight shone,
a girl who rose in sounds
above our commonness,
over our school's grey grounds
lilting and luminous---
wasn't she someone since
bowing in Milan,
awing the audience
at the Metropolitan?
The questionnaire goes out---
no one knows where she went---
so many singings shot
down to such silences.

JACK HENRY

Better in some ways, in other only equal,
he was one of the best players on the team,
with a Greek physique, and fast as panthers go,
a quiet smiler, someone in a dream.

Come on Jack, sleek co-eds proudly squealed
and pompoms shook and longlegged majorettes
tossed flickering sticks and caught them as they wheeled.
Jack made a touchdown and the band boomed for the Saints.

But glory's short and high school soon was done;
we all went elsewhere and Jack, too, couldn't stay
in spite of all the trophies he had won;
hanging around the Y, he'd had his day.

Then whether because he was black or maybe because
he lacked the luck on which so much depends,
Jack got a job as porter at the Elks Club,
keeping things neat for the fathers of his friends.

JOSÉ RAMIREZ

It was a comedown, after he had starred,
his calves in knots, cleating yard by yard,
not to hear the cheering of the crowd---
his heart still pumped, ready to explode,
waiting around for offers, going to L.A.
to the big games, smoking and drinking Cokes
now he needn't keep in shape to play.

He worked on a garbage truck, quit then hit the road,
but he came home to dance with his mother one bright day ---
a lady noted for her light tortillas,
she would be his cook, Rose and Juanita
wait on tables, serapés on the walls---
he saw himself being chauffeured in a Rolls.

And they did prosper, opened up more rooms,
hired an earringed cook whom José married---
their place is famous for its chili rellenos,
succulent tacos and hot enchiladas---
José hasn't forgotten the hopeful ball he carried,

he stands there friendly, ringing up the cash,
grown stout with time, but to remind him
how once in his golden youth he made a dash
toward high school glory over the winning line---
faded photos of the team behind him.

TOM WHITE

He had to wear that shoe
and steel around his leg
withered from its size---
handsome otherwise,
his walk a clogging dance,
and smouldering deep down,
ashes of bitterness

because he'd been a boy
who couldn't play the game,
his clodhop never chosen,
and had to bear hot pity---
"Too bad Tom is lame"
whispered down a corridor
by some bright lip of flame---

but tall as anyone,
normal except for that,
sang well, learned to swim---
married at twenty-one
a girl from Fullerton---
and when the war began,
requiring every limb
perfect for the march to death,
how many envied him!

THAT KID

That kid played soldiers still at seventeen,
lined up little lead men down in the dirt
(so emotionally arrested he later became
an Air Force Major--- death his lifelong work).
Always the hero or villain in school plays,
what he wanted to be was only an actor,
but some eternally adolescent factor
kept him from ever going beyond that phase.

If there hadn't been a war who knows who he might have been?---
a Burton, Brando or Olivier---
convincing in his parts, with a flowing face
he only had to command and it would harden
to a naive teenager or a man of grace;
there was a war, however, and for him
dramatic uniforms and guns and planes
to make of blood and murder, child's play.

LEON HENDRIXON

He didn't want to go
but wasn't it his duty?---
broad--- blond--- six feet two
(to giddy girls a cutie)
how could he nonconform?---
ticketed to camp
he got a uniform
and warned against the clap.

Learned to shoot a gun,
bayonetted dummies,
heard unpresbyterian
words like shit and cunt---
lined up more than once
drunk on a week end pass,
liras in his pants,
to rent a piece of ass.

And for a purple heart
exchanged an eye and leg---
he'd played his hero's part,
lucky to escape
with any of him left ---
he doesn't even lurch,
science is so adept
at surrogates that work---

you can't tell which eye's which---
his wife is svelte and pretty
and maybe less a bitch
than if she felt no pity---
he's glad to be alive
but wonders now and then
how little can survive
and still be called a man.

DAN ANDERSON

A lunchtime pal of mine,
big-eared, blond, blue-eyed,
except for friendliness
an undistinguished guy,
not much one for sports
or showing off onstage,
he was the audience,
though good at repartee---
happy with Bs and Cs
(Ds in Spanish 4),
Don Juan of Saturday,
he had a tomcat ease---
I heard him purr away
toward love, and then to war

and met him later, manager
of PAY LESS CUT RATE STORE
where once we used to eat,
bright noons of hope and peace---
older, darker, heavier,
friendly, though, as ever---
but different beneath
his open casual verve
(the cigarette he smoked
seemed a burning nerve)
as if he'd expected more
from life he loved so well
until at ripe nineteen
qualified to kill.

LEE ZORN

Four eyes, he was called, in Coke bottle bottom glasses
looking out like madness at us all---
and after stabbing several of us with pencils,
got tutored at home, forgotten until that fall
we started high school, when he too enrolled
and rolled his magnified eyes and lunged among us,
somewhat subdued, though just as odd a child.

He spent all period in a corner of the pool,
and disappeared beneath for a minute or so,
holding his breath, and gulping up through bubbles,
having viewed who knew what world below.

A genius at math, whatever his other troubles---
government scholarships sent him on through school.
Then World War II. He didn't have to go,

but stayed on campus; I saw him once on furlough
from the pacifist camp in which I'd been shut up---
shambling along, antisocial as ever,
armed in every pocket with pencils in rows;
years later noticed his picture in the paper,
banqueted and honored among those
who'd hatched the A-bomb by their mad endeavor.

C. B. "MATHEW" BRADY

Pictures were his life---
a bee's-eye meter hung
(as some boys wore a tie)
waiting to see the light---
in streets where victims moaned
he whipped his Leica out---
caught, at The Fiesta,
the sad face of the crowd,
dipped, where all glowed red,
contrast in the scene---
was it an Orange Queen?---
he analyzed the shine.
At war, snapped target towns
to show where death should dive,
and once at Buchenwald
shot bug-eyed corpses live.
But finally settled down
behind a Fourth Street lens---
passport photos, high school classes,
pictures of the bride.

JANET AND HOWARD DARLING

Both had dramatic flair
though cast in minor parts---
later, masked in mascara
who was that movie star
she looked like?--- Claudette Colbert?---
and he, usually a professor---
a bit in "Smilin' Through"---
sometimes a stuffy butler
with one good line or two.

And after they were married
and he'd come back from war
they organized a play group---
evenings of Williams and Shaw---
everyone thought her a wonderfully
convincing Blanche du Bois.

They didn't have any children---
both successfully taught,
but lived for their footlit weekends,
a Lunt and Lynn Fontanne
smiling down the rows,
at Playhouse and at Ebell
bowing to applause.

And when he had a heart attack
and couldn't do his roles
she donned her wigs and makeup
and braved the boards alone,
playing for him on the aisle,
cheering him up at home,
assuring him with that trick smile
the show, the show must go on.

ALL STAR

Rick Wayne,
swam, boxed, faded back
and spun the ball toward touchdown,
broke records, out for track.
He was a modest good guy,
maturer than his peers
and got our vote--- his genial teeth
flashed on down the years---
always with a "hi, there"---
he worked to earn those Bs---
in time of peace, won letters,
in wartime, stripes on sleeves.

Engineer or buyer,
his life turned out just fine---
a perfect son and daughter,
a house on Orange Lane.
And when his wife grew haggard
and then cut open, died---
he slowed enough to take
agony in stride,
a little sadder, maybe---
a truth for which he pined---
but to question Winesburg virtues
never crossed his mind.

Section Six: GAP

MY BROTHER MADE MODEL AIRPLANES BUT NEVER SNIFFED GLUE,

the only painkiller in our house was aspirin,
Uncle Peter drank, but only a beer or two---
when we wanted to escape, we went to a movie,
breakdowns were rare, addicts far and few.

Mrs. Johnson wouldn't come home by sidewalk,
strolled on parkway grass to save her shoes---
Aunt Glennie refused ever to see a doctor
no matter what the backache or the bruise
(and lived to be ninety one or two).

As for Aunt Nettie, any swearword shocked her
in spite of what the Bible might include---
you could have said, and truly, we were modest,
eccentric sometimes, seldom very lewd---
and mostly tried, in our way to be honest---

however, that was only half the truth---
books brought light to some, if slow and dimly,
and if the radio, beaming news of doom,
mostly made us laugh or buy Ipana,
it wouldn't be long before we walked the moon.

OASIS

Right in that desert burning
and barrenness we'd known
there was a pool of learning,
shaded, on a lawn---
thought--- art--- poetry---
that somehow bubbled in.

Not much of an oasis---
a college--- it was called---
but in such thirsting acres
we were waterfalled
and forested with furthermores
where aridness appalled---

every drop more precious
for being scarce outside---
Shelley--- cool--- delicious---
deeper hints of Freud---
almost surreptitious
but tasted and enjoyed.

Remembering as a gone mirage
that small green spot of mind,
some went on from there
and found a lusher land---
others, lost in blazing air,
adjusted to the sand.

GAP

At first a hairline but I felt it widen,
coming back from class I jumped the gap---
that world beyond me and the warm inside one
of knickknacks, Mom's applesauce, sweet orange pop---
the campus, under its slim trees, brick and green,
seemed to drift off farther every day,
harder to reach across a rift between
the block I lived on and uncertainty.
On one side, Plato, Darwin, Degas, Keats,
an updated cave waiting on the other,
cozy with everything a cave boy needs
according to his jungle dad and mother---
finally, to get back home across the chasm
I had to hang on tight and swing like Tarzan.

CITRUS HEIGHTS

Friends on Citrus Heights
(famed as a lovers' lane---
more than one young couple
descended into pain,
cheer leader, football hero
wished they hadn't lain
high on that hill of trouble)
we had only come
assigned to map the stars,
a few lightheaded students
getting out of cars.

Cepheus, Cassiopeia---
we scanned the twinkling dark---
put down the wheeling Dippers,
joking, on a chart---
the darting dogstar, Sirius
(Browning's "All that I know---?")
blue green red and silver
behind Orion's glow
of jeweled belt and scabbard,
and there blinked Betelgeuse,
the streetlight town below.

We laughed among the magnitudes
and showed them as a mark,
ignorant Ptolemaists
out on a freshman lark---
we searched and filled the circle
with Cygnus and the Crab;
and only much much later
would we feel the nights
slip from our selfish center
and know the sweetly bitter
distance of those lights.

EDWARD MORGAN BARRY

He once had played a gorgeous Romeo
to Madam Modjeska's delicate Juliet,
but now that he was sixty two or so
his nose had purpled and his face gone fat
and matinees had dwindled to a class.

How he sometimes strutted for us, though,
with his best side profiled, and as if
he still had something left that tights should show,
read a line like tossing us a gift,
deserved or not, of pure Shakespearean pearl.

OUR TOWN

The Windsor tie, the knickers that I wore
were a costume in a play that couldn't happen---
in the third act, I was a time warp corpse;
the rain that sounded real didn't dampen;
the girl playing Emily went through an invisible door.

I'd never lived in a town like Grover's Corners
and I felt much to modern to believe
the umbrellaed feelings of the simple mourners
really had anything to do with me---
those quaint New Englanders were more like foreigners

in a tintype time before anyone wanted to be
a tall and slangy movie hero kissing
lipsticked sophisticates on a solid screen---
Emily came back to the grave from her ghostly visiting
and said the living moved too fast to see

anything around them, and I agreed
watching in a theatre in a city
twenty seven years later, when instead
of whizzing through the present I was sitting
in our town, as it was then, among the dead.

DOUBLE DATE

We walked the Long Beach Pike,
four on a double date---
whirled and rollercoasted,
reflected back in black.

The others kissed and touched---
I only took her hand---
we watched the onearmed artist
sculpturing the sand---

I asked her if she liked
the bronzes of Rodin---
and then we went to look,
strolling on the strand,

at a fat belly dancer---
"And do you like ballet?"
We saw the dogfaced boy
and, twined behind a glass,

joined just at their waist,
pathetic siamese twins
forever face to face---
nature made me wince.

We walked the Rainbow Pier---
the others stopped to neck,
she shivered warm beside me---
I wondered what she'd think

if I clutched her like that,
but pointed out, instead,
the faint enormous swan cross
blinking overhead.

IN THE BASEMENT OF THE CARNEGIE LIBRARY

                                      where
poetry was kept
down in the dust, in the dark,
in the webbed and terrible air
someone-- was it I?-- sat writing a sonnet
right in the dim light of a librarian's stare.

Among the *Readers' Guides* and the yellowing pages
this brighteyed boy I wouldn't recognize
if we should meet on some more modern street
was putting down in rhyme iambic rages---
in a stretched syntax, with "thees" like Shelley and Keats,
penning lines for the ages.

The grey linoleum cracked, the table creaked,
the antique librarian seemed to be having a vision---
though it might have been only something she'd had to eat---
while I--- or this boy--- was coming to some decision---
whether 'tis nobler in the mind to suffer or try to write
one poem at least.

And I wasn't even aware as I paused my pen
where mummified golden glory mouldered beneath,
and the sphinxlike librarian glared as I sighed in my passion,
that it wasn't a sonnet I wrote in that old room
but was signing my life away, entombed from the eyes of men
like a Theban fashion

MRS. NORTHCROSS

She was a gentle, Chaucer loving lady
who made the paper Prioress alive---
small at the lecturn, but remembered lately
evoking in that room giants of delight---
Shakespeare with his black wired reeking mistress,
sensuous Keats coughing out his lungs,
Shelley flying in the mystic distance,
Byron nobly dying for Greek wrongs.

The grass itself began to show a difference,
the local trees became Wordsworthian---
no rose without Burns' red red inference

grew in the yards we'd called American;
we saw ourselves aslant through English eyes
and missed our edges that were Mexican
where darkness glinted with guitars and knives.

What did Blanche Trayo care about old odes,
dusting Spode in our white dining room
at a greenlawned bus stop far from her rutted roads?
But still in class the English lanes led on
past gothic tales, castles of indolence;
Mrs. Northcross skipped most of the modern---
it was too late for Eliot or those.

And scholarship is easy to condemn,
hanging us up like old hats on its traumas---
often on my couch I've looked back when
I sighed my sonnets, blind to social dramas,
about to curse those early verses, then
heard Mrs. Northcross warmly telling us
some of the best that has been known and said.

MLLE. SMITH

Her accent had the "n's" and liquid lips,
a gourmet seasoning suggesting streets
of plein air restaurants, tiny coffee cups,
the fountained Tuileries where lovers meet
near statues without clothes, and pigeons puff.

She rolled those "r's" out of a fleshy throat,
burbled and chirped and hacked as sensuous
as if in tête-a-tête Aux Deux Magots
she lifted absinthes with impetuous
Baudelaire or burning eyed Van Gogh.

And stood before all Paris with her stick
tapping at the bridges and the banks---
Les Halles with soupe à l'oignon hot and thick
(but didn't mention how the pissoirs stank)---
a woman middle-aged, whose tongue could lick

the sauce from any labial there was,
in a big hat, and dressed like yesterday
and never having been except that once
at the Sorbonne, more than a day away
from her mother's imperious mid-Victorian glance.

MISS BAGLEY

Slide after slide after slide
Miss Bagley pointed out---
proportion by the Greeks,
the balance on each side
of marble David pausing
forever there, surprised.

Van Gogh's gobs of field and sky,
Renoir's way with light,
Rembrandt, Rubens, Titian,
each one stroking clear,
with curve and cross and swirl,
aesthetic signature.

Art--- where line by line
the natural jut or mound,
the often graceless figure
becomes almost divine---
click--- and then Picasso
distorted what we'd learned.

But still Miss Bagley stood there
with a pointer on the slide,
her ruined face a lecture
as mirrored girls find,
that time is in the picture
and beauty in the mind.

JUDITH LOVELACE, M.A.

There was a teacher, proper and precise,
her lovers, in that sometimes loveless place,
neurotic Hawthorne or elate Mark Twain---
men of letters hers to entertain.
Was she ever lonely? Which of us knew?---
her wardrobe always coolly crisp and new
seemed put on to greet a James or Norris
whose ardent messages she quoted for us.

And where she went in that flat, flowered town,
she was accompanied by invisible men,
some who were elegant, some like rough Jack London
dashing forward brash and wildly sudden,
with whom she had incessant dialog,
smiling brightly as she walked along
at dark obscurities of meaning in

a word they'd chosen or a comma's hint.

What else was there?--- love's disappointment,
family madness behind her eyes' sad glint?---
if so, she never said--- glasses on a ribbon,
she read a poem of Frost's, warm with wisdom,
asking us the reason in the rhyme,
class after class, hair whitening with time,
reverer of values, cherishing the word,
learning's mistress, not there understood.

DR. TYGER

Our only PhD,
he had a missing thumb---
too far and fierce of thought
for college in our town---
he taught philosophy
in the face of our ho hum.

Assigned: "What I Believe,"
my essay prayed to God
for which I got a C
that first warm autumn term---
Plato and then Nietzsche---
the worm began to turn

minerals in the mind---
and all that rainy winter,
worked on underground---
Spinoza, James, Descartes---
seeds were churned around;
our hungry looks grew thinner

as he held, with his absent thumb,
logic before our class---
atheist or cynic---
whatever that Dr. was,
like Socrates he had to leave,
accused of corrupting us;

assigned again before he did
(Scotch, not hemlock drunk)
a later springtime Credo
for which my A summed up,
ending in doubt, leafy wonder's
blossoming begun.

FIELD TRIPS: GEOLOGY 1 & 2

We read the book of earth,
how heavy paged it was,
the document of rocks,
the record in the cave---
crystal sentences,
paragraphs of stone---
strata that contained
words of fern and bone---

drove out to pen a note
on chapters of the past---
a mountain starting molten,
now a snowtipped cone---

the writing of the rivers,
erasures done by sand---
scanned the glacial eons
it took to make a grain---

and singing "Clementine"
on highways leading home,
we felt how far we'd come
from what we hadn't known

and how the story took us
on field trips into time
instead of back to dreaming,
farther from the slime.

MRS. OATES

A smooth poetic pearl
in every phrase she said,
who would have thought she'd ever
mistakenly go to bed
with such a rawfaced roughneck,
the man who growled "he don't,"
we saw waiting for her
sometimes after class,
his lineman's gloves in his pocket,
whiskers on his throat---
"Oh, Mrs. Oates, Mrs. Oates,
how could you have done it---

versed in Blake and Browning,
have married a brute like that,
who climbs prosaic poles
only to fix the wires
connecting telephones?"
But we were green aesthetes then,
idealistic youths---
so many precisions we didn't guess
in non-intellectual pursuits.

SOCIAL CONSCIENCE

The novel I was writing for creative writing
concerned the gap between the rich and poor---
since I was neither, it required some research---
trips to L.A. in Dan Anderson's rackety car.
The daughter of a Pasadena millionaire
(we wound past Spanish mansions fanned with fronds)
would fall in love with her hard up chauffeur
(we gawked through treeless streets of stunted homes)---
I bought *Das Kapital*, *The Grapes of Wrath*
sang "The Internationale" through orchards back toward town---
then wrote a searing social paragraph---
but next we asked some laughing girls along,
and the middle-class turned out to be such fun
I never did get far past chapter one.

ROSEMARY OR JASMINE

There was an acned girl from the south---
I can't recall her highly scented name---
Jasmine or Rosemary--- with a painted mouth
that smiled and smiled
though she was slightly lame.

Toward groups on lawns or laughing after class
she'd lurch with books and looks of friendliness,

under the ginkgo, come and sit with us
and show her knees
below her checkered dress.

No one liked her--- even with those breasts.
When she intruded, the bright sun seemed to spot---
you felt her fingers would have smeared the tests;
once she appeared
for reasons we'd forgot

we'd have to leave, and left her on the grass
or in the room, sucking at her beads
and thinking who knew what?--- that we were crass?
as if to see her
were to feel diseased.

One day in the library she screamed upset---
what was the matter, either with her or us?
What did she have to do, or be, to get
better grades and friends
and elected to clubs?

The librarian, like a tigress, growled and hissed
and pawed her overdues and snarled and paced
to see among the lucky and the kissed
the lonely mirror
she too had faced.

RICHARD McGREGOR

Exciting, urbane, he came to our backward acre,
breathing of books, with whiskey on his breath,
as much only young as he was a conscious faker,
and less a fellow of flesh than man from a myth,
he didn't belong, that glamorous Richard McGregor,
sad as an exiled prince
in our insular midst.

Ulysses, perhaps, anchored at some little island,
the light of horizons glinting in his gaze,
suggesting a Siren hurt by the smile of his silence,
taking whatever we gave but not meaning to stay,
he played at our picnics, bored but pretending compliance,
dallying there
until he could get away---

and what he became, after he left us forever,
none of us heard--- though I too moved from that place,
and once, at a distance, thought I saw Richard McGregor
prosperous bellied, older, balding and grey,
the undistinguished uncle or businessman father
of any he scorned as a friend
in his interesting day.

MARYJO MALONE

Some of her lines and some of her sonnets
might vie with Shelley's she had such a sense
of meter and of which words went together---
like Browning, she had found an eagle's feather
somewhere past the pasture's barbed wire fence,

but she was modern, too, wrote free verse
and had a summer affair with Richard McGregor,
who gave her sex, but not his next address---
she followed him into Berkeley's mist jeweled weather,
worked in stores for a while, and went to night school,

learning how to shape and fire a pot,
then moved back down to where she'd been a fool,
and though she no longer thought of herself as a poet,
her successful ceramics had a lyric anguish
and women came from miles to browse in her shop.

THE FAMOUS POET

She came on drunk in red velvet---
it was the end of her tour---
a marriage breaking up,
new certainties of war---
her poems suddenly didn't seem
important as before---

she hammed them, played the great

Bohemian from New York,
threw the lines away,
thirty years of work
and what did it add up to?---
a college whistle stop.

Nothing she wrote or thought
prevented history---
those listeners in their rows
guiltier than she
of ignorance and hate,
pettiness, bigotry.

She thought of lips she'd kissed---
no one had loved so well---
and all it had done was lead her
deeper down this hell ---
she laughed, wildly, mid-poem---
hiccoughed, almost fell,

but in her bourgeois audience
past mists of alcohol,
some girl--- or boy perhaps,
waiting--- watching her veer---
to take the torch from her tired grasp
in Iowa or here.

CHALICE

Memory, that old magician's mixture,
has me down in the grass and throbbing in clover---
as green as I was--- I'm watching myself in a picture
of candlewarm buds, the gone world's would-be lover.

Merlin--- God himself--- or whoever it is---
spring's morning sorcerer and good at grails,
has led me shining on and led me back
through sunfloating sycamore groves to the hillside trails
beside a snow cold stream in the land of the lost.

Dropped from a hidden cup of pain and joy
there is a meadowlark song like a gem in the grass---
and I bleed as I break through the steel webs of the past,
nude to the waist, Lancelot's pure boy
seeking illusion's chalice to the last.

THE STREAM

Somewhere out of time
I'm sitting with her now
on the same stream rock we sat on
leaves and lives ago.
Right where we waded out
and sat with a dazzling book
in the Heraclitan flow ---
she looks at me and I look
away at the swooping line

of the hillslope and the blue
curve we're moving in,
at the sycamores that blow
faintly in the wind,
and down where our bubbling feet
look sculptured in the foam ---
then at her side's light touch
a hardness rises up ---
we're turning into stone.

We're marbled there midstream ---
carved in a changing flow;
I feel her lean and lean,
I sense the mosses grow.
I'm sitting with her now
holding the mottled book,
our stone feet in the gleam,
our look a lichened look
lit by the speeding stream.

WHEN NO ONE ELSE HAD EVER BEEN EIGHTEEN

I tried describing in the later air
the way it never was but might have been
when no one else had ever been eighteen,
lovers, who didn't even know we were
lovers, laughing underneath the leaves
along the road from somewhere into summer,
walking among sweet whiffs from orchard trees ---

she pushed the bike beside my swimming knees,

Steinbeck in the basket whom we'd read
loafing in an oleander shade
and blow a storm of dandelion seed
and feel each point of greenness blade by blade ---

that was the way it was I tried to see
but there were bugs like motives underneath
whenever, sighs from then, I tried to say
it really was so bright and grass so green ---
the seeds of freeways blossomed eaten grey,
Steinbeck showed sold colors on a screen.

FEELING SURREAL

Feeling surreal, I lifted a phone of ants ---
my old hat wore a rusted   Willkie button
and at my wrist a timeless wristwatch dripped.
Outside, the apricot had blossom faces;
I sat passé and listened to her voice,
witty and glib, although the record scratched ---
illumination like a light through grass
moved on the walls where winking eyeballs watched.

The phone kept burning in my moaning hand ---
I wavered in the warp from now to then,
a Blake-faced father to tell me I'd discover
not much later she was not the one
I thought I spoke to in my fool's confusion ---
but just before the melting phone went dead
I kissed the nipple of a cruel illusion,
and armies of ants marched off with my lost head.

FROM AARDVARK TO ZYMURGY

My Uncle Peter was determined
in those less wordy days
to make himself more learned ---

so started out with aardvark
and worked right through the A's.

"All the books there are to read
I've read," I heard him say ---
"with beer and sandwiches in bed ---
histories, mysteries, modern fiction
while your Aunt Lillie lay
snoring in her coldcream."

"I don't!" her wrinkles claimed.

"Of Mice and Men?" I asked him ---
but that was a mistake.

His eyes in their red rims
and wart began to blink ---
"He's one of those pink socialists
who writes about life's stink."

And even Shakespeare wasn't
what the critics think,
Lamb's *Tales* an improvement,
livelier, more succinct.

The centuries of art dismissed,
I almost dropped my drink
of ginger ale Aunt Lillie brought
in on a tray of birds.

"Uncle Peter, have you thought --- ?
Couldn't you have missed --- ?"
but after he'd reached zymurgy
there were no other words.

HEIGHO SILVER

"I think it's just wonderful --- you keep at it ---
my favorite poets are Shakespeare and Edgar Guest --- "
I was urged on by my literary aunt
in whose house, though she had confessed

to poetry, I noticed books
were scant,

whereas my father, who had once read Zane Grey,
told me, as "The Lone Ranger" heighoed Silver again,
that there wasn't any money in poetry
and advised, as the masked man galloped through radioland,
"Why don't you try writing
something like that?"

One cousin who had graduated from high school
and been forced to memorize "Thanatopsis"
but who wasn't completely opposed to poetry nevertheless,
reading one of my early efforts said
it must be good because it made her
think of death.

While the word-clever girl I went steady with ---
and I wasn't ever sure exactly what she meant ---
grinned cryptic critiques which I could interpret
(she felt she knew how touchy even would-be poets get)
either as a budding Shakespeare
or an overblown Edgar Guest.

And a young teacher at college listened politely then mentioned
she too had gone through a phase ---
every English student has ---
or thinking herself a Shelley or an Edna St. Vincent Millay,
but --- like acne or indigestion ---
assured me it would pass.

And soon I was able to, I moved away from that place
and the longer I didn't live there, the listier it got
with little schools and steeples and orchards stretching out ---
its emphasis on money gradually forgot,
until its far illiterate face
seemed more kind than not,

and I went on writing poems, right through war and TV
even when I found anti-art and bad taste
weren't limited to towns of ignorance dreaming half asleep,
and even after I saw, looking back with a pang,
those dead wouldn't rise up into the light
whatever poets sang.

As soon as I was able to, I moved away from that place

Section Seven: REMEMBER PEARL HARBOR

PLACES EVERYONE,

                        yesterday's set is now ready,
there's a chair called Director but no one knows where he is,
someone in charge is scowling over the book ---
the microphones hum, cleverly planted as flowers,
streets, buildings, houses, hills are painted to look
red gold at sunrise and change with the changing hours.

The actors go through their parts, they are rapidly aging ---
a parade flickers by of later and later cars ---
a sensitive boy from a novel walks hand in hand
with a girl by the groves as the colors and angles improve ---
they go not far from the sea in a palmed promised land;
the leaf trembling town is viewed through the lenses of love.

In these scenes you see them laugh as they listen to music,
the banktower's clocks and churchspires pointing above ---
a scent wafts, of lemon and salt, through incredible blue
almost too pure --- it really needs some adjustment ---
the trees and longstretching lawns are too green to be true ---
those virginal urges they feel should have an encrustment

of freudian lust not to appear unreal ---
but much that's been hid by these fronts is already shifting,
a harmless era comes to the end of a reel ---
the town is a screen in a wind that pulls and is lifting
until where it flaps as it blows you can see underneath
these pictures that glimmer and charm, a whole world drifting,

political figures with bombers and troops behind ---
clearer and clearer the town begins to be seen
not as it ever was but a town in the mind ---
the lumber where dreams were tacked on is starting to lean,
the faces themselves, under masks, are harder to find
and some, without make-up, look more and more twisted and mean;

flags flap from all the front porches, at blacked out windows
dagger sharp stars of gold slice from their frames ---
men crutch back legless, stare eyeless, tear swollen widows
forget like the rest and dance out in dresses like flames ---
gone, too, in that wind, the earlier innuendoes,
those who died for nothing are nothing but names

on which obscurity thickens; the native returns
no longer out of a novel or young at his lines ---
he's poking for hints that elude in the paved over ferns,
trying to find the gone town where freeways wind,
and finally drives off forever, that lover, that son
toward a skyline of shadows cast on another time.

THE ONLY TROUBLE

        "Si jeunesse savait, si vieillese pouvait"

Someone said in my dream you don't look forty
and I smiled like my tinted high school annual picture,
my blond hair bleached on a beach,
flattered to blandness where nothing ever happened ---
a town around me, stucco to my touch,
the safe streets arched by blossom purple trees.
The only trouble was, I was asleep.

Pater familias among the breathing bedrooms,
and teen prince strolling in a town of dreams,
both at once, I passed the ghostly peacocks
of sprinklers on the lawns and whistled along
now past the courthouse with its flag and cannon,
now past the churches whose crosses seemed to mean,
shining from steeples, Christ hung in the scene.

Someone came up to me and said you don't look forty
and I smiled my tinted smile of seventeen.
My thought caught throat couldn't scream a warning ---
"None of it's true, this pre-war town's a dream."
I ran through the town to find my sleeping children.
I wanted to shake them awake to what they must learn.
The only trouble was, they hadn't been born.

COMMUNION

Welch's Grape Juice --- and I'm prousted there ---
to Christ blood Sundays tinkling in the trays,
a hymnbook incense hovers on the air
where flesh was spongy Wonder Bread we ate,
symbolic cannibals, I in my teens,
pimpled and slicked, and talcumed not to reek.

The ritual is sterile, quick and neat.
We take the cruel communion's crustless pill
good Presbyterians cut behind the scenes
and now His body's eaten, wait until
the minister says "Drink ye all of it"
and wash His murder down with something sweet.

OUR WORLD

Aunt Nettie said Norval would roast in hell
for calling Richard a fool, my father
switched me, a crimewave at nine, for shouting goddamn ---
some words weren't in print although I heard them,
none of us there ever pissed or shat.

Movie husbands and wives slept in twin beds ---
in real life, if it existed, guiltily screwed ---
as for anatomy, we were pallid dolls
with clothes contrived to hide whatever looked lewd ---
everyone passed away but no one died.

Nothing but shameful statues in Greece and Rome,
naked baths and geishas in Japan ---
disbelievers of truth, we liked our world
and really thought our duty was to save it ---
no one as sure as aunts who stayed at home.

NORWALK

Whenever we went past Norwalk it was a joke ---
"I guess I'll have to stop and let you all off here,"
Dad said, or, at any odd opinion:
"Norwalk's where you belong --- "
We never knew exactly what they did there,
the crackpots, the loonies, the mad wife from next door,
but on our side of the fence, we laughed secure,

sane in our fears and foibles while they were crazy ---
we seldom screamed at midnight or tore off our clothes ---
there was a wall past which we didn't dare,
and if we wandered regions sometimes hazy,
we soon came back into the normal air.

When everyone went berserk --- that was called war ---
and F.D.R. told God He was on our side;
we fought for peace, and killing wasn't murder,
the only thing we had to fear was fear

but it seemed to me --- though of course I was much younger
and didn't know how right a wrong can be,
that lies are sometimes the truth, and the line is a fine one
dividing the irrational you from the lucid me ---
that someone like Dad had let us all off at Norwalk
and the wide open gate no longer had a key.

REMEMBER PEARL HARBOR

When America entered the war, my mother blamed
everything on my father --- screaming in the kitchen
he was a Hun, a Nazi, a Dutchman, and furthermore
responsible for every new invasion ---
Austria, Poland, France, England and now ---
hadn't he hired that Jap once as a gardener? ---
Pearl Harbor.

She shrieked Murderer murderer murderer
at my meek father transfixed at the sink,
accused, too, his head of being square.
It was the worst Christmas Eve that I remember
and when I couldn't help crying, they both turned
and said, "What does it have to do with you?"
"What are you crying for?"

But I seemed to go on and on crying forever,
though they went on just as they had before ---
he passed communion in church, Christian as ever
and after she'd stopped being bitter
she cooked sauerkraut and wieners again
and other dinners of forgiveness she thought
fit for her Hitler.

STEVE YAMAMOTO

Because our names were always at the end,
as boys sometimes become in nearby seats,
I was his and he my schooltime friend ---
we pledged allegiance to the starry states
with liberty and justice (not yet under God)
and sang sweet land, and learned important dates ---

and then, as time and school went on and on,
his delicate face shone out in every class ---
an intellectual, though a witty one;
in some trim garden at the edge of town
his toylike parents bent to vegetables,
prideful of their slangy, nisei son.

"Why do you have to drag God into every poem?"
he asked me once, one eyebrow cynical ---
a twinkling critic, and though I was hurt,
who thought my verses brought down from a pinnacle
where they'd been writ by lightning, word by word,
compared to his bright haikus, they were absurd . . .

we argued, still good friends; and then went on
to Berkeley's broad green campus and white spire
booming *jucundum* as red suns slid down
behind jeweled bridges and the bay on fire ---
the wide wide world and most of it to learn,
infinities of knowledge toward which we could aspire.

But one dark day the bombs of madness dropped ---
oh my God --- it can't be --- they can't have done that! ---
freedom, equality, America suddenly stopped ---
democracy was cancelled from the map,
and my friend Steve, a slanteyed bucktoothed Jap,
got locked up in a concentration camp.

EDGAR NELSON

Waving the latest little scrap of hope,
his father rushing from his Fourth Street store
showed some passerby his son still lived,
pointing out his stance, or the ring he wore.
See, he'd say, he has a nose like that ---
he made it to Bataan --- Edgar's alive ---
and raised the glass above the hazy picture,
a bigger blur when dots were magnified.

And I could see him, too, but in the Mojave,
panting up a dark red lava slope
to the top of Pisgah, where our class had climbed
to study soda caves in the burnt out cone,
or laughing in my room as we boned for tests,
and suddenly serious thinking of Europe's war ---
he told his plans and hopes for love and work
and all the joys and times life had in store.

We talked the pros and cons of peace and war,
and he as much a pacifist as I
dreamed the day when violence would cease
and men be friends instead of cruel and sly,
and he came by one last bright Easter Sunday
in brilliant buttons, tall and bravely creased,
and glad he needn't worry about the Nazis,
sailed with the peacetime army toward the East.

MY SUDDEN COUSIN, MY SANGUINE MINISTER,
AND THE CRUELTY OF CONVICTION

My sudden cousin, short on the glorious Fourth,
held a bomb too long and exploded his hand ---
blood all over, several stitches worth,
a bandaged hero, but to his Dad and aunts
more fool than valiant, little boy than man ---
time, and World War II took care of that.
He shot up fast and filled a uniform
in a plane with a gun that went ratatatat
to zoom on German housewives, neat and fat,
hanging up windy wash on Monday lines.
"I saw bright blood on the white sheets," he wrote,
"making little splattering designs ---"
and aunts, Dad, Congress, smiled with pride
to have my sudden cousin on their side.

My sanguine minister kept us up to date
with hopeful views in pacifistic sermons ---
lions and lambs, and how the swords of hate
might forge to pruninghooks in spite of Germans
gassing more Jews, and, tuned to Über Alles,
goosestep troops down Paris avenues;
Christ died upon the cross of human malice,
loving the world, a glory we should choose.
But when JAP SNEAK ATTACK was all the news
hot, bloody voices leaked through radios,
my sanguine minister harangued the pews
with also apropos though different quotes ---
Onward, Christian Soldiers --- the thing to sing ---
a sword, not peace, was what Christ came to bring.

She felt conviction was a cruel thing
--- what would we do if everyone refused? ---
a hawk flew by on slow and slanting wing,
I walked beside her frown like one accused.
Flayed eucalyptus hung in wounded autumn;
we strolled by ditch ice on the country road.
The world of sunset had no top or bottom.
Her given hand was cold and mine was cold.
I said she might be right, but what we'd do
was live in peace, no matter what the reason.
War couldn't be if every man said no.
We saw the rabbit's guts, the hawk's hooked feeding ---
softness torn by bloody beak and claw.
Beak in my heart, I felt her hand withdraw.

CONSCIENTIOUS OBJECTOR

When I told her I was a conscientious objector
she said how could you do this to me?
interpreted my idealistic defiance
as a no to her personal war.
She'd like to have waved me away into battle
and while I was wading in gore
she'd be sitting under the apple tree
knitting sox for the Red Cross

with some nearsighted 4-F. Nevertheless,
an Emersonian believer in self-reliance,
I chose life not death ---
though if it should have come to dying
I'd rather have died for the truth ---
not that I thought I had such guts,
but refusing to kill anyone, even for her,
seemed next best to being nailed up.

FIRES

So inexpressive that they might have been
New England Puritans standing stiff as starch
for formal portraits glaring out at sin,
my family seldom kissed, and held back touch ---
their fires of feeling had to burn within,
their hidden lives sometimes turned to ash
though to the world they still looked much the same,
plainfaced with platitudes, and never rash.
But I remember once Aunt Emma came
crying brightly at me, "Wie geht's, Liebchen?"
and kissed me less as nephew than as man ---
and still am scarred by that encounter when
my mother clutched me --- with a mouth like flame ---
and begged me not to go away again.

DRESSED FOR AN OCCASION

Coiffured, she looks alive,
hymned asleep on satin,
yet wouldn't nap so dressed ---
she would have had a hat on
for church, frilled in her best.

Where is her dimesized watch
with its darkblue jeweled winder
and digits I used to read,
her onetime time reminder ---

and why is her finger freed
of its diamond engagement
to him, who creaks in a seat
with tearspots on the suit
she always kept so neat?

Glad for such pink glads
at any other time
and wreathes and banks of roses
instead, deaf to the tune,
hands crossed, she reposes

waxenly indifferent
to whatever Dad forgot ---
whether the blinds are down
and the cat has been put out ---
nearer to God or not.

EYES

When I went home to watch my father die,
he'd shrunk to almost no one, cut and tubed,
but in the lasting blueness of his eye
I saw a man still young and strong with youth.
He took my hand, as he had seldom done
upright in his pride of time and place ---
but now that he was dying he held on
crying as he smiled to see my face ---
anxious even then for my well being,
though he lay almost gone, and doped from pain ---
reflecting back the son that he was seeing,
as in an equal inner eye of mine
I saw my son, but in his shining eyes
nothing yet of those eternities.

BROTHERS

If one of us had come from another planet,
maybe we'd have been still less alike ---
tiger and housecat, taloned hawk and linnet,
"as different," they said, "as day and night" ---
how he would hum, and buzz an inlaid table
and scoff because I couldn't saw a line ---
if he had been a sibling in a fable,
I'd have been his Abel, brained in time ---
but actual brothers aren't so Karamazov ---
fiction likes to touch up blood and tears ---
and show how God brands Cain and warns him off,
but east of Eden, kinder with the years,
he fixes houses for his son and daughter,
and for my children, I make poems here.

NOW THEY WORK IN BANKS

Mrs. Northcross said ---
One I thought as talented
as Carl Sandburg's dead
of alcohol in an accident ---
and that's the only thanks
an English teacher gets.

I taught them Browning, Keats ---
I tried to do my best.
Oh but I'm proud, so pleased
you weren't like the rest ---
and there's another, too ---
I praise God for that ---
who's publishing like you.

I should get up and dance
for two who've stayed in flower,
yet what about the ones
I had in every class ---
those three or four with power
to turn the common greyness
into a gorgeous phrase ---
withered in an hour?

Where's Maryjo Malone
whose "wings of a white bird flying"
were light as any flown
on winds of Shelley's sighing?
What's Alan Eastman done
who once without half trying
tossed off a villanelle
and fleshed a sonnet's bone?

Maybe it doesn't matter ---
perhaps it's just as well ---
I'm not really bitter ---
I hope they still read poems
and when your volumes sell
theirs will be the homes
that have them on a shelf ---
those small town mute inglorious
Miltons, like myself.

OOHING THE UMLAUT

Oohing the umlaut, I was reading Dog Years aloud
to Mrs. Northcross's nineteen-forty-one class
and all the dead and greying were a crowd
of sophomore faces in the rose-cheeked past ---
but I kept losing the place, flipping through
the Nazi parable by Günter Grass.

I wasn't prepared to get up there like that
several wars later, a reader of the future
and find the passages to tell us what
was going on in Deutschland at the time
when there were football battles to be fought
and college bells had such a pretty chime.

Really surreal --- in fact, it was a dream ---
but which one was, I wondered, losing the place ---
my middle age paging for the line
or the waiting audience with its unlined face,
and Mrs. Northcross smiling sweet as cream
in the back row, ready with her A's.

I doubt if she'd have given Grass that grade
if he had come before us as I did
to read to the class that hadn't died or greyed
our certain fate from a dream book that said
wake up, say no --- it isn't yet too late ---
before this sleep becomes a nightmare state.

1938 ---

The breakfast room table was set ---
familiar underfoot,
a dog I reached to pet ---
I turned the radio on ---
Charlie McCarthy joked ---
a twist, and deep blue flames

petaled on the stove
to warm the cocoa up.

It was as if I'd come home
and everyone else gone out
somewhere for a minute ---
time passed --- where could they be?
the cocoa was getting a mold,
a fine dust settling down,
F.D.R. came on
to say Pearl Harbor'd been bombed

I waited --- I fooled around ---
handled things on the mantle,
the shepherdess' web-cracked gown,
chipped candlestick, pink candle ---
the radio went mad,
mentioned an atom bomb ---

the cocoa had eaten the spoon
and still they didn't come home
the dog I reached to pet
felt like wagless bone

the mirrors had sprouted a beard
my diaries turned yellow
out in the bulldozed yard
a skyscraper started to grow

I heard them ringing the chime
I wanted to let them in ---
"Harold, it's us, we're home!" ---
everything inside
broke and began to festoon ---
the way in or out was blocked ---
"Harold, why is it locked?" ---

the paranoid radio told
men were off to the moon ---
"Harold, open the door" ---
then with a deafening roar
as if it had never been
the walls of the dream caved in.

I FIND TIME

Getting rid of things, I find time
deep in my desk, the very Elgin watch
my father gave me --- nineteen-thirty-nine ---
as I took off my graduation cap ---
it told me when Jack Benny would come on
and then how long until my Shelley class.

There was a girl sitting on my lap ---
it ticked against her nipple in the dark ---
it clocked the mountain endlessness of camp ---
against Ann Arbor snows, glowed like a spark;
I wore it to an Oakland wedding once ---
on summer's wrist it left a winter mark.

It had an hour for fatherhood, a hand
that never moved while I did boring chores ---
but went right on, band by changing band
into the fifties, circling in its course
until I slipped the dim past off at last
and tried to put its fastness in a drawer ---

but now I've wound it up again I've found
its jewels still work, its springs still coil and run
the wheels that fit the wheels that turn around
pointing out that nothing has been done
either to speed it up or slow it down
since smiling at time, I youngly strapped it on.

AUNT ANNA MARIE HAYES

                        was no Lily Pons ---
her upper registers quavered
but she sang on, sang on
for family, friends and neighbors ---

sometimes high Ced in solo
in the choir at the Methodist Church ---
intoned "He was despised"
under their gothic arch,

warbled "O promise me --- "
at nieces' and nephews' weddings
and cleft The Rock of Ages
in sadder settings ---

struck dumb when Uncle Harry
was sealed where he couldn't clap,
she found her voice again
and practiced while she gasped
between the doctorings
for what had long been wrong ---
then even with much cut out,
rose on wings of song.

When Melvin went, and Elva,
she stood against stained glass
evoking with wrinkled lips
the Rugged Cross ---

and daily in her nineties
alone in that little house
last roses bloomed behind,
facing a captive audience
deaf in their frames all around,
birdlike, almost blind,
still made a singing sound.

GOLDEN WEDDING

This couple in the picture ---
what they could have told
of vanished pioneer times,
the wagons toward the sun ---
births without a doctor,
fragile sapling groves ---

of tragedies and faiths ---
the nine who long survived,
the laughing girl they lost ---
of heatwaves and of frost ---
goateed, cameoed,
two from a righteous past

who here look joyless, quaint,
their era over with
of grim squarejawed endurance,
sobriety and grit ---
Michael and Sarah Witt
whose ghosts are in my bones.

LATER

There we were lives later ---
it hadn't changed so much;
we biked down dream back roads
then passed the well kept fronts ---
Bush St., Broadway, Sycamore
flickering with lawns
under the St. John's bread trees ---
all the mothers' sons
wheeling through the shadows,
headed into town ---
the clear air sweet with lilac
brushed by wings just flown ---
we passed the sandstone courthouse,
a cannon on its grounds ---
we pedaled past the Elks Club
to noontime churchbell sounds,
but when we got to the center
--- hey, Ma, look, no hands!
the signs said DO NOT ENTER ---
all it was was sands
between the windowed canyons,
hovered by a hawk;
we got off, grown men,
and walked our bikes along
among the playing tumbleweeds
and plate glass raying webs ---
desolation whining
like wind through whitened ribs ---
feeling terror crawl our spines,
our bone hands clutching rust
as slowed spokes crumbled, and our names
blew away like dust.

HOME MOVIES AT NEWPORT

She says if they could rise up from their graves
and see your handsome family here at Newport
growing and grown ---
her eyes show childish movies of the years,
quick generations dragging sandpails out ---
The young one looks like you did then not now ---
the waves break background green and do not change.

She sits there in her seventies at least,
lively survivor of so many dead ---
uncles rocking on the album porch,
the watermelon brightness of the Fourths
when winking seeds flecked Grandpa's silver beard,
the little house spilled cousins out the doors
before the rumors of the wars were heard.

Fat rich Frank a penury of bones
and laughing Jack a black and soundless grin,
Elva, too, and Oscar, Melvin, Joe,
a list of ghosts comes back to sun and swim.

She doesn't like my beard. It makes her old,
and glasses, too --- has youth gone dim so soon?
How many times since then this sea's unrolled
rolled back and stayed the same, cruel changeless coast.

She almost slaps a thigh but doesn't quite;
enthusiasm wrinkles, not yet lost ---
she had to see the children in this light
against the curving summer sound of foams
before the coming winter --- and that night.
Goodbye, goodbye, Aunt Nettie. Yes, I'll write.